■

Confirmation
Wars

HOOVER STUDIES
IN POLITICS, ECONOMICS,
AND SOCIETY

General Editors
Peter Berkowitz and Tod Lindberg

OTHER TITLES IN THE SERIES

Warrant for Terror:
Fatwas of Radical Islam
and the Duty to Jihad
by Shmuel Bar

Fight Club Politics:
How Partisanship Is Poisoning
the House of Representatives
by Juliet Eilperin

Uncertain Shield:
The U.S. Intelligence System
in the Throes of Reform
by Richard A. Posner

Preventing Surprise Attacks:
Intelligence Reform
in the Wake of 9/11
by Richard A. Posner

Confirmation Wars

Preserving Independent Courts in Angry Times

Benjamin Wittes

HOOVER STUDIES
IN POLITICS, ECONOMICS,
AND SOCIETY

Published in cooperation with
HOOVER INSTITUTION
Stanford University • Stanford, California

ROWMAN & LITTLEFIELD PUBLISHERS, INC.
Lanham • Boulder • New York • Toronto • Plymouth, UK

ROWMAN & LITTLEFIELD PUBLISHERS, INC.

The Hoover Institution on War, Revolution and Peace, founded
at Stanford University in 1919 by Herbert Hoover, who went on
to become the thirty-first president of the United States, is an
interdisciplinary research center for advanced study on domestic
and international affairs. The views expressed in its publications are
entirely those of the authors and do not necessarily reflect the views
of the staff, officers, or Board of Overseers of the Hoover Institution.

www.hoover.org

Published in the United States of America
by Rowman & Littlefield Publishers, Inc.
A wholly owned subsidiary of The Rowman & Littlefield Publishing Group, Inc.
4501 Forbes Boulevard, Suite 200, Lanham, Maryland 20706
www.rowmanlittlefield.com
Estover Road
Plymouth PL6 7PY
United Kingdom
Distributed by National Book Network

First printing, 2006
12   11   10   09   08   07   06   9   8   7   6   5   4   3   2   1
Manufactured in the United States of America

British Library Cataloguing in Publication Information Available

Library of Congress Cataloging-in-Publication Available
ISBN-10 : 0-7425-5144-X (cloth : alk. paper)
ISBN-13 : 978-0-7425-5144-2 (cloth : alk. paper)

⊗™ The paper used in this publication meets the minimum requirements
of American National Standard for Information Sciences—Permanence of
Paper for Printed Library Materials, ANSI/NISO Z39.48-1992.

It was the best of times, it was the worst of times. It was the age of the courts, it was the age of contempt of the courts. It was the epoch of professionalism, it was the epoch of partisanship. Judicial power was never more secure, the judiciary was seldom more threatened. American constitutional law was never a matter of greater consensus, it was seldom more ferociously contested. Judicial nominations were of unparalleled quality, they provoked unprecedented political warfare. And to all sentient people of both parties, it was clearer than crystal that things in general could not be otherwise and that it was all the other side's fault. It was the year of Our Lord two thousand and six.*

*If apologies to Mr. Dickens are warranted, they are hereby offered.

CONTENTS

■

CHAPTER 1

■

Introduction

"Can it be different?" Chief Justice John G. Roberts Jr. asked rhetorically. "Of course it can be different. If there are serious questions about qualifications, senators should explore those. If there are serious questions about ethics, senators should explore those. If there are disputes about appropriate judicial philosophy and approach, talk about those. But barring that . . . everybody doesn't have to think that this is an opportunity for them to be the reincarnation of Clarence Darrow."

It was mid-afternoon, January 13, 2006, the day that the Senate Judiciary Committee wrapped up its hearings on Judge Samuel A. Alito Jr.'s nomination to the Supreme Court. I was sitting on a couch in the chief justice's office — the couch on which President John Quincy Adams, as Roberts cheerfully related the Supreme Court lore, had died.[1] Roberts was reflecting on his own recent experience going through the process of Senate confirmation. The chief justice was not complaining. He stressed upfront that "it's hard to look back on something that kind of worked out all right and say that there was something too wrong with it." Indeed, Roberts knows well that in the grand scheme of things, he has no cause for complaint. Nominated during a weak period of President George W. Bush's tenure, he nonetheless garnered confirmation on a comfortably bipartisan 78–22 vote. Opponents kept smears on his character to a minimum. He shined during his confirmation hearings. He emerged unscathed. On the surface, at least, the process worked just fine.

Yet Roberts clearly does not regard the process with satisfaction, either. And why should he? The modern system for confirming Supreme Court justices and many lower-court judges plays rough, as he well knows, his earlier confirmation proceedings having been famously rocky. President George H.W. Bush initially nominated him to the U.S. Court of Appeals for the D.C. Circuit toward the tail end of his presidency, but the Senate never acted on the nomination, which lapsed when President Bill Clinton took office. When the current president then renominated him in 2001, it took him an additional two years to win Senate approval.

Even under the best of circumstances—and Roberts's nomination to the high court was just about the best of circumstances for a conservative nominee in the current environment—the modern process thrives on unpleasantness and aspires constantly to pressure nominees to make promises concerning the substance of their coming jurisprudence. So Roberts, an establishment lawyer who has not regarded himself as a culture warrior or a political combatant, saw ads run against him that were, he felt, "beyond the pale," particularly one that linked legal arguments he had made as a government lawyer to a bombing at an abortion clinic.[2] He saw press inquiry into his personal life that he regarded as "wholly inappropriate."[3] While he generally seemed tolerant of the hearings—describing them at one point as "a very real moment" and "in a real sense exhilarating"—some of the questioning troubled him. The senators, he said, "had particular concerns. They want you . . . to say something about areas of concern to them under oath. The idea obviously is that, having said that, you then go forth to your new position and act accordingly." This problem becomes particularly acute during the so-called "courtesy calls" nominees have to pay on senators, individual visits that provide yet another opportunity for senators, this time in private, to press their special concerns and lobby for specific outcomes.

"There's no reason to suppose that [a judicial confirmation] couldn't be a very uplifting, educational, informative discussion about—however you want to phrase it—the role of the courts [or] the appropriate judicial philosophy. . . . People don't have to view it as a grilling or a cross-examination, or an effort to come upon a gotcha moment. . . . Maybe that's overly idealistic, but I don't know why it should be."[4]

Roberts's wish does indeed sound hopelessly idealistic, so far removed from the reality of the modern nomination as to be a happy, civics-class dream. Nominations to the high court today represent major political confrontations, grand mobilizations of the political bases of both parties, along with their affiliated interest groups and sympathetic academics. Even lower-court nomination battles can get exceptionally ugly. It was, after all, filibusters of circuit court nominations that almost brought the Senate to a standstill in 2005. The combatants in these battles do not understand themselves to be engaged in an uplifting, educational discussion. They are, rather, fighting a form of political warfare: One side wins, the other loses, and the blood left on the ground detains neither.

Yet the chief justice poses a fascinating question: Why exactly does the confirmation process function so brutally? Could it, in fact, be different?

In some respects, this is a strange moment for all-out political warfare over the courts. Today's Supreme Court, the fulminations of many conservatives notwithstanding, is not the Warren Court.[5] While the justices have not backed off the rights revolution of earlier eras, neither have they, for some years now, generally been in the business of aggressively creating new individual rights.[6] Nor, the fulminations of many liberals notwithstanding, are Americans living through an era of aggressive conservative jurisprudence.[7] True, the high-court majority has revitalized a long-dormant concern for state power and property rights and has curtailed its earlier liberal enthusiasms—and some conservative jurists would go much further. But unlike the infamous *Lochner* era, in which the justices used constitutional law to remove huge swaths of regulatory policymaking from the purview of legislators, one struggles to identify the great areas of liberal policymaking that have been placed off-limits by any modern constitutional doctrines. The threat the Court poses to conservative values, in other words, lies largely in its refusal to overturn opinions it issued long ago—on abortion and on church-state separation, particularly—not in new innovations today. Its threat to liberal values, by contrast, lies chiefly in things it might do in the future. In contemporary political terms, the Court functions neither as a consistently conservative nor as a consistently liberal bastion but as a decidedly middle-of-the-road actor—arguably representing the center of gravity of American political life better than both President Bush and either party's caucus in either house of Congress. The public recognizes this. In Gallup polling over many years, strong majorities have expressed confidence in the judicial branch, and a plurality has regarded it as neither too liberal nor too conservative.[8] Yet in the strange paradox of modern judicial politics, the American political system has chosen this time to wage a truly unprecedented war over the courts.

At first glance, the Roberts and Alito nominations—along with the ill-fated nomination of Harriet Miers—suggest that the toll this war has taken on the president's ability to place qualified people on the courts has been limited. Roberts and Alito, after all, were both highly qualified nominees, and on that basis the Senate confirmed them—though Democrats had substantial ideological anxieties about both. The process may not have been pleasant, but pleasantness is not democracy's function. Those opposed made their case, and the Senate—after examining the nominees' qualifications, background, temperament, writings, and ideology—gave its consent. The president got his men, who were, significantly, precisely the sort of people he had promised in two campaigns to put on the high court. So the public got what it voted for. No great procedural machinations materialized to stop the nominations— no successful filibusters or major manipulations of committee rules. Interest groups made a lot of noise, but so what? That is their job.

By contrast, Miers, the White House counsel, was far less obviously qualified to serve on the Supreme Court, and the confirmation process brought out bipartisan anxiety about her background, her judicial philosophy, and the apparent cronyism of her appointment. As a consequence, she never made it to a hearing. The cumulative lesson would seem to be that quality matters and that ideology matters somewhat less than many observers had imagined.

All of this is true as far as it goes and yet fails to capture the full dynamics of the recent nominations. For one thing, it ignores the increasingly partisan nature of Senate votes on nominees. Only quite recently, nominees like Roberts and Alito would have been confirmed with near unanimity. If one leaves out Clarence Thomas, whose confirmation was clouded by Anita Hill's charges of sexual harassment, the twenty-two votes cast against Roberts actually exceed the combined "no" votes cast for all of the other seven justices sitting at the time of his confirmation. And this understates the matter; many Democrats swung in Roberts's favor only at the end, in the wake of the surprise decision by the Judiciary Committee's ranking minority member, Patrick Leahy, to support him.

Roberts could easily have received many fewer Democratic votes. That is precisely what happened to Alito, whose forty-two "no" votes made the party-line nature of current Supreme Court voting far clearer.

Put simply, everyone knew before either man was nominated that a partisan fight would take place the moment President Bush announced a name.[9] Everyone knew Democrats would reflexively oppose the nominee. Everyone knew the arguments they would make—tailored, of course, to whomever the nominee happened to be. Everyone knew further that Republicans would support the nominee in virtual lock step. And the process played out, within a reasonable margin of error, exactly as everyone had expected. In other words, while the process may have worked in the formal sense, it also reinforced the trend of recent years toward highly partisan consideration of nominees, and it moved America closer to the day when party-line votes are the norm for high-court nominations even in the absence of substantial allegations of misconduct or unfitness. Indeed, after the Alito vote, one should probably say that this day has arrived.

Nor can one honestly describe the hearings on either nomination as deeply informative. Both, rather, were dominated by a Kabuki dance so oft-performed it has grown meaningless—a dance that merely to describe is also to ridicule. A Democratic senator asks about one controversial case area after another—dwelling for unnaturally long periods on abortion. The nominee tries to make reassuring noises while saying little and committing to nothing. The senator waxes exasperated. The nominee insists he will merely follow the law. The senator points out that different judges have different views of the law. The nominee mutters something about bringing no agenda to the job. Eventually the clock runs out. Then a Republican senator professes indignation at the questioning and lobs softballs at the nominee for his allotted time. Then the cycle begins anew with another Democratic senator. At most, senators and viewers received some sense of Roberts and Alito's personalities and temperaments. But surely nobody can confidently predict their judicial behavior based on their performances at their hearings. Surely their hearings added little to what senators and the general public could glean from their written records and long careers. Exactly what did anyone learn? Indeed, what did anyone expect to learn? The honest answer is that Americans learned very little that would responsibly inform a vote on their confirmations—and that is exactly what everyone expected.

Concluding that the process works based on President Bush's three Supreme Court nominations of 2005 is a mistake for another reason: focusing too narrowly on Supreme Court nominations obscures the larger judicial confirmation process. The high court, after all, constitutes in numerical terms only about 1 percent of the federal judiciary. Because its nominations have always been more contentious than lower-court picks, it is possible, though I think rosy, to see more continuity than change in the way the Senate considers Supreme Court confirmations. When one examines lower-court nominations, where the change has been more dramatic, the shift—along with its negative consequences—becomes more obvious.

It also becomes more obvious when one watches the process up close, from the point of view of nominees, rather than from the point of view of a political culture debating an issue or set of issues that has somehow come to be embodied in an individual. My personal experience as an editorial writer for a major newspaper has shaped my views of this subject considerably. I have covered innumerable confirmations across two administrations of opposing parties. The formal protocol of nominations forbids judicial nominees from speaking to the press, but the reality is that many of them—and many judges, for that matter—quietly do so anyway. I have frequently contacted nominees the *Washington Post* was considering supporting or opposing. As a consequence, I have had an

unusual view of what the process does to people, how it can mis-
characterize them and render binary scores—left or right, good or
bad, liberal or conservative—out of complicated and subtle minds.
A good example here is Miguel Estrada, a highly credentialed
Washington lawyer whose nomination to the D.C. Circuit Democrats filibustered to defeat on the grounds of his supposedly extreme right-wing views. Estrada is, indeed, deeply conservative, yet
his politics and legal views are hardly simple. He opposes the Supreme Court's decisions of late revitalizing the commerce clause
as a limitation on congressional power relative to state governments, for example—one of the cornerstones of the conservative
judicial revolution. Yet, just as he declined on principle to give
his views on abortion during his confirmation, he felt constrained
not to express his views on this subject though they might have
reassured some senators.[10]

I have also watched how senators seek to extract the crudest of
concessions from people who are supposed to function as independent judges. One of the earlier cases I covered involved President Clinton's nomination of William Fletcher to the U.S. Court
of Appeals for the Ninth Circuit, a court on which his mother,
Judge Betty Binns Fletcher, already sat. Keen to prevent too many
liberal judges from getting confirmed, Republican senators trotted
out an obscure anti-nepotism statute and argued that Fletcher's
confirmation would be unlawful unless his mother stepped
down.[11] Fletcher's nomination was held up for three-and-a-half
years. Even after the elder Judge Fletcher did, in fact, agree to take
senior status following her son's confirmation, conservatives—including then-Senator John Ashcroft—continued to block the nomination. Slade Gorton of Washington even managed to force Clinton to name a Ninth Circuit judge of his choosing before
Fletcher's nomination—along with a new addendum to the anti-
nepotism law—finally moved.[12]

Even when things go well for a nominee, the process is grueling and unpleasant. I talked and e-mailed with Roberts several times while his nomination was pending. He remained generally cheerful throughout, but the stress on him was clear—and he is far from alone. Most judicial nominees are not political figures who have become used to the spotlight or to having the details of their lives spilled out and flyspecked. Many have never regarded themselves as controversial in a partisan sense. My point here is not to condemn the process for being mean—though it surely can be that. Were it nasty in pursuit of genuine insights into a nominee's likely performance on the bench, its nastiness would be defensible, if regrettable, and one could reasonably ask nominees to endure it. Yet senators and interest groups—and sometimes the press as well—have an unfailing tendency to focus on marginalia and irrelevancies, often quite painfully for the nominees, while getting the big picture wrong. Fletcher, after all, has been a fine judge. Estrada, I firmly believe, would have been as well. The nastiness, in short, seems to serve no democratically ennobling— or even useful—function. If Alito did not know before his nomination which "side" he was on, I venture the guess that he has a pretty good idea now—as his letter of thanks to the social-conservative group Focus on the Family suggests.[13] Somehow, the Senate has created a confirmation process in which it learns little that is useful while pressuring would-be judges to conform to the wills of legislators who do not themselves agree on what results they should demand of nominees. Along the way, it probably imprints upon them a stronger partisan identity than they had prior to nomination and charges a sometimes exorbitant personal toll.

Why has this shift taken place? How did judicial nominations come to be political battlegrounds in the first place? Is the change, as I have suggested, really for the worse, or is it perhaps better this way, more democratic in the sense of open to the broad array of voices in a diverse society? Should one understand the nastiness of the process merely as the rough-and-tumble of politics or is something deeper at stake—and what might that something be? Why do Americans fight so tenaciously over who serves on their courts?

Broadly speaking, contemporary political and academic debate offers four answers to these questions. The first denies either that fundamental change has taken place at all or that the change causes real problems. Nominations are political and always have been political because the judicial function itself is political, this argument goes. The second school, which is orthodoxy in conservative circles, holds that the process has changed fundamentally and puts the blame for it squarely at the feet of liberals and Democrats and their alleged tendency to seek policy results, rather than honest adjudication, from the courts. The third approach, orthodoxy in liberal circles, acknowledges the change and blames it on alleged right-wing court-packing by Republicans. A final school of thought laments the change and apportions blame for it evenly between the parties, seeing it as part of a larger pattern of diminished civility in American political culture. Each of these four schools embodies important elements of truth, yet none ultimately proves satisfying.

My purpose in these pages is to offer a more complete explanation of the changes to, and the decline of, the process of confirming judges over the past several decades. Put simply, any reasonable account of recent history compels the conclusion that the process has changed dramatically—and for the worse. The change has played out differently in Supreme Court nominations than it has in lower-court appointments. At the Supreme Court level, where the spotlight constantly shines, stalling for any long period is politically impossible, so in purely procedural terms, the system still works pretty well. Nominees are voted on in a comparatively timely manner, and ideological clashes over nominees take place overtly—with senators using the process to put pressure on nominees for substantive concessions. At the lower-court level, where public attention slackens, the process itself has broken down more completely; nominees may garner little vocal opposition yet simply never receive a hearing or a vote. Appearances notwithstanding, though, these changes represent different symptoms of the same degenerative condition: an ever-increasing Senate fascination with its ability to control access to the bench.

Yet in contrast to ideological commentators, who insist on seeing this change in partisan terms, I shall argue that one should understand it principally in institutional terms. The process has deteriorated steadily regardless of which party has controlled the White House or the Senate. While it has worked better during periods of unified government than during periods of divided government, any improvements have inevitably failed to stick over the long term: Lower-court nominations take as long now, in a period of unified Republican control, as they did at the end of the Reagan administration, when Democrats controlled the Senate. Both sides piously insist that their hands are clean, and each manipulates the data to show how the other has transgressed. In one sense, both sides lie; they are both guilty. But the bipartisan nature of the guilt suggests that the blame game itself is somewhat misplaced. That is, driving the deterioration of the process is something deeper, something more tectonic, than mere partisan political hardball.

One should, rather, understand the rise of Senate fights over nominees as an institutional response on the part of the legislative branch to the growth of judicial power in the years since the Supreme Court handed down *Brown v. Board of Education* in 1954.[14] The court reinforced this response with its subsequent rights revolution, which continued into the Burger Court years and culminated in *Roe v. Wade*.[15] The judiciary's increasing assertiveness has taken place against a much longer-term democratization of confirmation politics, driven both by constitutional change and technological developments. Confirmations evolved from a closed debate among unelected senators before the ratification of the Seventeenth Amendment in 1913 to a process broadcast live on national television since 1981 and still more recently dominated by interest groups with abiding stakes in the specific manner in which the judiciary wields its power. The shift in confirmation norms has also taken place against a backdrop of increased partisan polarization in general, as the political parties have evolved from broad umbrella organizations focused to a great extent on patronage into more consistently ideological animals.

Some reaction to the astonishing aggrandizement of the judicial role in American political life over the past five decades surely followed inexorably from the bolstered judicial role itself that began so dramatically with *Brown*. Indeed, while many commentators—generally but not exclusively conservatives—decry the big footprint of the courts in modern America, judicial power is actually a matter of greater political consensus than these commentators like to admit. Both parties want certain things from the courts, and for all the worthy rhetoric about judicial restraint, jurists across the political spectrum have shown themselves willing to act aggressively to overturn considered judgments of Congress and state legislatures. Over time, this tendency has placed a great premium on the Senate's gatekeeping function of giving the president its "advice and consent" for his nominees.[16] That function's scope has ballooned accordingly.

Yet though some change perhaps could not have been avoided, the increasing aggressiveness of the Senate's conception of its function poses significant challenges for maintaining independent courts over the long term. The problem, I shall argue, has both concrete and speculative dimensions. In the immediate term, the extortionate quality of modern confirmations, in which senators make their votes explicitly contingent on reassurance by the nominees about substantive areas of concern, creates a Catch-22 for the nominees—a burden, I shall argue, of which we should relieve them. More broadly, one must worry at least a little bit that the increased aggressiveness of the Senate in this area is the thin edge of the wedge. That is, the norm of a relatively non-adversarial confirmation process was only ever a norm, not a constitutional requirement or a matter of law. It was, however, a norm rooted in concern for preserving the independence of the federal courts. And several of the other major protections the judiciary has against legislative insistence on substantive outcomes—budgetary pressures, impeachments, and jurisdiction-stripping measures, most particularly—are similarly mere norms. In the long run, the breakdown of the confirmation process may represent a leading indicator of a far larger effort by the legislature to rein in judicial power.

Unlike the chief justice, I no longer harbor any particular faith that "of course [the process] can be different"—if by different he means less ideological. In my view, rather, the tectonic forces that have moved the American political system to this point will strongly conspire to keep it there, indeed, to push it further down the road on which it has set off. The real question is how to manage the political conflict surrounding nominations so as to protect the independence of the courts and the prerogative of the president to choose judges—as well as to maximize the utility to democratic government of the Senate's more aggressive, ideologically oriented approach to its role. To this end, I shall argue for several steps. Most importantly, it is time to revisit the value of having nominees testify before the Senate Judiciary Committee. This practice, which is of relatively recent vintage and quite disreputable pedigree, has become the ugly centerpiece of most contested judicial nominations. Yet the hearings—because of the irreconcilable conflict between their ever-increasing ambition to explore a nominee's soul and the appropriate reticence of nominees for a judicial role to bare their souls—almost inevitably prove an embarrassing spectacle that yields minimal information. Getting rid of nominee testimony and forcing senators to vote on a nominee based on his or her record and the testimony of others would by no means eliminate nasty nominations fights. It would, however, let a good deal of the air out of the balloon—eliminating that one extended, nationally televised moment at which senators publicly name the price of their votes. By contrast, we should accept the legitimacy of certain senatorial efforts to pressure the president to name ideologically acceptable candidates, pressure of a type far more aggressive than the Senate typically contemplates today. The broad idea is that in periods of divided government the Senate ought to focus its considerable power on forcing the president to nominate someone to the majority's liking, rather than waiting until the president has made his choice and then pouncing on that person.

This essay proceeds in four parts. In the first, I examine several common explanations for the modern judicial confirmation process and attempt to illustrate both their strengths and blind spots. I then turn to my own theory of the process's decline: that, notwithstanding its partisan mask, it actually represents an institutional response by the Senate to ascendant judicial power—judicial power that both broad political movements alternately decry and revel in. In the third section, I consider the concerns the modern process poses for an independent judiciary. I conclude, first, that, in the context of confirmation hearings, the conflict between the nominee's necessary reticence and senators' desire for answers has become unsustainably acute and must be addressed. Beyond that discrete issue, I argue that the broader consequences the process threatens are, at this stage, still largely speculative but, given the trajectory of the process, potentially ominous over the long term. In the final section, I offer strategies for managing the conflict, focusing particularly on ending our failed experiment with nominee testimony and in shifting the Senate's energy toward more honest and effective confrontation with the White House.

CHAPTER 2

■

An
Unsatisfying
Debate

The first major school of thought on the change in the process of judicial confirmation is denial—or, at least, a jaded understanding that the process has always been thus. This attitude is somewhat muted in public debate but common in academic circles. Its most prominent recent articulation is that of political scientists Lee Epstein and Jeffrey A. Segal, who put the matter bluntly: "the appointments process is and always has been political because federal judges and justices themselves are political."[1] Epstein and Segal acknowledge that there have been changes in the modalities of the struggle for political control over the courts. "[N]ominees to the lower courts now garner scrutiny once reserved for candidates to the Supreme Court, and interest groups and the media are paying even more attention to Supreme Court nominees," they write. But their concession is narrow. For them, the continuity in the process eclipses the changes to it. "[W]hat has not changed," they contend about both Supreme Court and lower-court appointments,

is that, almost without exception, presidents from the early years
of the United States to the present day have sought to exploit
vacancies on the bench for ideological and partisan purposes.
Senators have done much the same, supporting or opposing
nominees who help further their own goals, primarily those that
serve to advance their chances of reelection, their political party,
or their policy interests. This was as true of John Adams and the
Senate of 1800, which attempted to pack the courts with Fed-
eralists in order to advance their own interests, as it is now of
George W. Bush and the Republicans in 2005, who desire a
federal bench replete with conservatives.[2]

At the core of this argument lies the notion that the judicial
function is so indelibly political as to necessitate a highly political
appointments process. Epstein and Segal note that "until judges
and justices stop reaching political decisions, the process will never
become any less political." Yet they wave away the possibility that
courts have ever been, or could ever be, in the business of ruling
based on neutral principles. Responding to conservative suggestions that a return to respecting the will of the Framers would
remove the courts, and thereby confirmations, from the political
heat, they write: "We say there is nothing to return to. Political
decision making and political decisions started in 1800, not in
1953 with the 'modern' Court."[3]

Few articulate this thesis quite as boldly as Epstein and Segal,
yet the broad proposition that the political nature of the process is
connected to the political nature of the task of judges pervades
much contemporary commentary. Judge Richard A. Posner, for
example, writes that it is "no longer open to debate that ideology
. . . plays a significant role in the decisions even of lower court
judges when the law is uncertain and emotions aroused. It must
play an even larger role in the Supreme Court, where the issues
are more uncertain and more emotional and the judging less constrained."[4] Posner describes the confirmation process as reflecting

the broad social recognition of this unprincipled reality. "The evidence of the influence of policy judgments, and hence of politics,
on constitutional adjudication in the Supreme Court lies every-
where at hand," he writes. "Consider the emphasis placed, in confirmation hearings for nominees to the Supreme Court, on the
nominee's ideology to the exclusion of his or her legal ability. I
don't believe a single question directed to then-Judge Roberts in
his hearings for confirmation as Chief Justice was designed to test
his legal acumen."[5] Put crudely, the argument is that constitutional
law is now, and always has been, merely a mask for the exercise
of political power; politicians know this and act accordingly, as they
always have.

An important variant of this argument does not seek to deny
change itself but denies instead that the change has caused real
problems. In his deeply challenging defense of the modern Supreme Court confirmation process, political scientist Michael
Comiskey candidly acknowledges the changes to the process over
recent decades—and celebrates them. In light of the "constitutional schism" of modern times, he writes, it is "well that greater
power sharing by president and Senate in the Supreme Court appointment process has come about, and is likely to grow, by placing
more clearly on the shoulders of the president and his nominee
the need to prove the nominee's suitability for a seat on the Court."
Comiskey dismisses as overwrought criticisms by legalists, who fear
a politicized process, and criticisms by politically oriented scholars,
who fear that the process is ineffective in exposing the views of
nominees. The process, in fact, is "normally well-functioning," he
argues. Americans tend to have a pretty good sense of who their
justices are going to be. And conflict over nominees who are arguably "unqualified, unethical, or politically extreme" is both "predictable and healthy."[6]

The first virtue of the denial argument, in my judgment, is its
non-ideological character—that is, it does not seek to describe the

process in terms of the impropriety of one side or another but rather as a struggle for power among competing political movements and branches of government over time. Moreover, I cannot argue strenuously against the proposition, at least with respect to Supreme Court nominations, that a great deal has not changed in the process. Epstein and Segal are certainly correct that there was no Golden Age in which presidents considered only merit in their selection of justices, whose confirmations senators considered with politics far from their minds. Nasty, overtly ideological confirmation battles did not start with Robert Bork's nomination in 1987.

The denial argument also correctly identifies the relationship between the institutional work product of the courts and the degree of friction in the confirmation process. The simple historical reality is that the contentiousness of confirmations has ebbed and flowed in direct proportion to the degree of public controversy surrounding the Court's work. So when President Herbert Hoover nominated Charles Evans Hughes to be chief justice in 1930, at a time when the Court was energetically striking down economic regulations in the name of substantive due process and other doctrines, the nominee faced fierce and overtly ideological opposition. By contrast, only a few years later, the confirmations of Chief Justices Harlan Fiske Stone and Fred M. Vinson, nominated in 1941 and 1946, respectively, took place within days of the Senate's receipt of their names and without significant debate of any kind.[7] The chief difference was that in the intervening years, the Court had backed off its aggressive stand and was not making itself a player in the central political issues of the day. In short, the denial school rightly recognizes that the history of this process is not a morality tale but, rather, a political power struggle loosely calibrated to the political culture's comfort level with the courts at any given moment.

These virtues conceded, the theory in its hard form goes way too far. That is, the belief that there has been no fundamental change in the process seems to me unsustainable. As I shall detail later, the process now takes dramatically longer and subjects nominees to often-overt, substantive pressures that would have been quite unthinkable only a few decades ago; the nature of the Senate's inquiry into nominees is far more intrusively probing far more frequently. Citing examples of contested or ideological nominations in the past proves only that the break with that past is not total. It does not begin to explain why today *every* Supreme Court nomination produces either an ideological confrontation or a huge public sigh of relief.

Moreover, the notion that the modern process for lower-court nominations is anything other than a radical departure from past practice seems to me empirically indefensible. In spots, Epstein and Segal seem to concede as much, noting the novelty of the "increasingly elevated and public battles over lower court nominees." But they see this change as limited, rejecting, for example, the notion that there has been "an escalating reliance on ideology and partisanship on the part of senators and presidents" with respect to the lower courts and insisting that it "would be a mistake to conclude that politics, in the form of ideology and partisanship, plays a far greater role in the 2000s than it did in, say, the 1930s."[8] I do not mean to romanticize the era of President Franklin Roosevelt's court-packing plan; the judicial politics of that period were certainly raw. But this just is not true. Republicans during the Roosevelt administration did not systematically block the appointment of liberal circuit court judges. The parties were less ideologically polarized then; patronage played a larger role in judicial selection than it does now.[9] And the data simply do not bear out the contention that partisan politics then pervaded lower-court judicial confirmations as thoroughly as they do today.[10]

Comiskey's notion that the contemporary process, for all its occasional ugliness, actually possesses many virtues is more challenging. Indeed, a good deal of the instinctive revulsion the process induces is rooted less in any discernible harms than in its appalling aesthetics—that is, in one's sense that a great democracy ought not embarrass itself every time it wishes to put a justice on the high court. Comiskey's argument is a powerful reminder that, at least at the high-court level, many of the harms attributed to the process remain somewhat speculative. The trouble with his contented approach, however, is that it underestimates the acuteness of the problem the modern system poses for nominees, a problem that only grows more acute as political polarization pushes toward routine party-line votes on nominees. By focusing only on Supreme Court nominations, moreover, Comiskey actually misses the full severity of the problem, which is often greater at the lower-court level, where public attention lapses. No senator today, after all, would dare demand the resignation of one justice as a condition for the confirmation of another, as Republican senators did with Willie Fletcher's nomination to the Ninth Circuit, for example. And for all their talk, Democrats did not launch a serious filibuster effort to stop either Roberts (against whom they launched none at all) or Alito (against whom they launched a nonserious one), though they have repeatedly filibustered circuit court nominees.

The various threads of the denial argument, in short, correctly caution us to avoid viewing the process as decaying as a consequence of somebody's partisan malevolence and challenge us to eschew hysterical overstatement of the concerns about the contemporary system. But they do so either by seeing greater continuity between present and past than actually exists or by underestimating the perils of the current path.

By contrast, modern conservatism denies neither that the change has taken place nor that the change contains perils. Rather, it bemoans the shift and offers a decidedly partisan explanation for it: It's all liberals' fault. Examples of this thesis are too numerous to detail, and its major themes—which I blend together here in a mélange that may not precisely reflect any individual commentator's view—are so oft-repeated as to have a familiar ring: Confirmation politics used to be a comparatively peaceful, ignored ideology, and focused on professional qualifications, because society at large agreed that the role of the courts was merely to interpret, not to make, the law. Then, starting during the era of the Warren Court, liberals turned to the courts to effectuate policy they could not achieve using traditional democratic means. Liberal judges departed from the law to deliver these results. And when conservative presidents sought judges who would return the country to more honest adjudication, liberal senators and interest groups viciously opposed nominees who would not swear allegiance to an evolving Constitution whose meaning at any time liberal elites could redefine. The watershed event was the fight over the Bork nomination in 1987, when Democrats defeated a manifestly qualified scholar for purely ideological reasons. The mendacity of their tactics has only escalated since then, culminating in the filibusters of President Bush's circuit nominees. As legal historian Stephen Presser puts it: "For the first time in memory, in public, one political party, the Senate Democrats, has taken the position not only that judges should be picked based on their preference for designated outcomes in cases that might come before them, but also that the Senate ought to be an equal partner in picking judges and that nominees who come before the Senate have a burden of persuading sixty Senators (the number necessary to cut off debate in the Senate), that they are worthy of ascension to the bench."[11]

The conservative critique often ends with an exhortation that only a return to politically neutral—that is, originalist—jurisprudence can deescalate these wars, which commentators often describe in apocalyptic terms. As the martyr himself, Robert Bork, writes, "The Court has converted itself from a legal institution to a political one, and has made so many basic and unsettling changes in American government, life, and culture that a counterattack was inevitable, and long overdue. . . . The leaders of the Democratic

Party in the Senate are making it the party of moral anarchy, and they will fight to keep the Court activist and liberal. The struggle over the Supreme Court is not just about law: it is about the future of our culture."[12]

In the conservative narrative, Republican mistreatment of President Clinton's nominees either did not happen or did not amount to much—certainly nothing compared with what Democrats have done during the current administration.[13] Excesses, in any event, were defensive, not ideologically based opposition of the kind that Democrats engage in now but the blocking of proponents of "judicial activism."[14] In short, as Justice Antonin Scalia nicely encapsulated the conservative critique in a 2005 speech, "If . . . we're picking people to draw out of their own conscience and experience a new Constitution with all sorts of new values to govern our society, then we should not look principally for good lawyers. We should look principally for people who agree with us."[15]

A softer, more sophisticated version of the conservative critique appears in an as-yet-unpublished book by conservative scholar John R. Lott Jr.[16] Lott begins with the refreshing proposition that both sides have blood on their hands, rejecting, in other words, the notion that the fight has been all one-sided. "Each side claims to be blameless while trumpeting detailed lists of the other's transgressions," he writes. And "[b]oth sides are right when they say their nominees are delayed longer and more often than before. Bill Clinton's nominees were held up more than nominees from prior administrations were, and George W. Bush's nominees have been harangued even more than Clinton's nominees." Lott also advances the intriguing theory that the "best and brightest" of both parties "are among those most likely to be derailed."[17] In addition, he brings to the table a wealth of useful data—data to which I shall return later.

Yet if he departs from the conservative orthodoxy on the nominations blame game, he falls solidly within it on the origins of the problem. "During almost the entire twentieth century, the Senate looked strictly at the three factors of competence, propriety, and temperament," not at the nominees' political views, he writes.[18] That changed during the Reagan administration, culminating in the Rehnquist and Bork confirmation battles: "The lesson for the Senate was that it was acceptable to make ideology an explicit consideration in judicial confirmations. The rules had changed."[19] The reason for this shift? "The liberal approach of going through the courts to get policy results that were unobtainable through the legislatures or by changing the Constitution is largely to blame for the increasingly nasty and prolonged judicial confirmation processes," Lott argues.[20]

The conservative narrative contains several important truths. First and foremost, many liberals *are* concerned principally with achieving or protecting specific results from the courts and will tolerate just about any judicial methodology to get them. Indeed, the Right's psychoanalysis of the Left—at least, of substantial elements of it—on this subject is largely accurate. Liberal law professors—who constitute a substantial majority in the legal academy— devote huge amounts of time to defending legally indefensible propositions and criticizing those reluctant to accept them for their supposedly cramped visions of the Constitution. For many activists, the confirmation process is nothing more than an opportunity to exact loyalty oaths to *Roe v. Wade* and other sacred cows. For many liberals—even for dominant liberal opinion—the spirit of Justice William Brennan and the energetic judicial Left has utterly defeated the spirit of Justice Felix Frankfurter and his reluctance for the courts to enter into the "political thicket."[21] There simply is no difference for them between their policy preferences and the requirements of the Constitution—and the function of the courts, to put it bluntly, is to stand and deliver.

The conservative narrative also correctly identifies the correlation in modern history between the threat perception among liberals and the tenacity of the fight. That is, when the Court was solidly liberal, the confirmation of a conservative such as Warren

Burger as chief justice could go off without a hitch.[22] Now, with the courts more finely balanced, with precedents liberals hold dear apparently more vulnerable, and with conservative judicial policymaking a real possibility, that does not happen. Rather, liberal opposition to conservative nominees has escalated as conservatives have approached a governing judicial majority on the central legal questions of the day.

But the conservative version of the story suffers from at least two major flaws. First, while conservatives properly diagnose the results-oriented fixations of liberals, they frequently fail to see the same disease in themselves. That is, conservatives reflexively formulate their own position as advocacy of judicial restraint, but in fact they often advocate not a more restrained judiciary but just a different set of priorities for the deployment of judicial power. Take, for example, Bork's own scathing bill of particulars against the modern Supreme Court:

> The justices have weakened the authority of other institutions, public and private, such as schools, businesses, and churches; assisted in sapping the vitality of religion through a transparently false interpretation of the establishment clause; denigrated marriage and family; destroyed taboos about vile language in pub- lic'otected as free speech the basest pornography, including com- puter-simulated child pornography; weakened political parties and permitted prior restraints on political speech, violating the core of the First Amendment's guarantee of freedom of speech; created a right to abortion virtually on demand, invalidating the laws of all 50 states; whittled down capital punishment, on the path, apparently, to abolishing it entirely; mounted a campaign to normalize homosexuality, culminating soon, it seems obvious, in a right to homosexual marriage; permitted racial and gender discrimination at the expense of white males; and made the crim- inal justice system needlessly slow and complex, tipping the bal- ance in favor of criminals. . . . Whatever one may think of these outcomes as matters of policy, not one is authorized by the Con- stitution and some are directly contrary to it.[23]

Leaving aside the merits of Bork's complaints, not all of them accuse the Court of having created rights that do not exist or otherwise overruled democratically elected political actors. Some, in fact, make precisely the opposite accusation: that the Court has *deferred* to Congress on matters involving campaign finance reform and affirmative action.

On the issue of property rights, conservative columnist George F. Will has candidly acknowledged that the conservative movement has hoped "judicial activism would put a leash on popularly elected local governments and would pull courts more deeply into American governance to protect the rights of individuals."[24] More broadly, he criticizes what he terms the legal Right's "dogmatic majoritarianism—the right of majorities to have their way," and insists that there exist "impeccably conservative reasons for regarding judicial review as a valuable restraint on majorities, and hence for having high regard for some judicial activism."[25] I dislike the hackneyed terms "activism" and "restraint," which mean so many different things to so many different people as to have little objective meaning at all. But Will seems to me to describe the standard most conservatives—Bork included—actually advocate in practice, if not in their rhetoric. That is, they, too, have their bottom lines, in the service of which they want the Court's power exercised. They are less different from liberals than they imagine.

More fundamentally, it is quite wrong to claim that ideological opposition to nominees is something liberals pulled out of the air during the Reagan or Nixon administrations. If the denial school errs in claiming that confirmations were always as fundamentally political as they are today, it does not follow that preceding the Bork nomination was some Golden Age of merit-based confirmation. Indeed, while the Bork nomination was a watershed of sorts, it was less of one than many conservatives believe. For while the degree of mobilization of public and academic sentiment and political energy certainly had no precedent, Bork was far from the

first nominee to face opposition, even to get rejected, on ideological grounds. Although he suffered some nasty smears—as well as
some fair criticism of a very long record of controversial writings—
he was by no means the first in that either. Bork, as I shall show
later, was not the first nominee to get Borked.

The truth is that no sharp break in 1987 separates an ugly
ideological present from a past in which senators of all stripes voted
regularly to confirm worthy nominees and refrained from consult-
ing those nominees' views in assessing their worth. The change has
been subtler than that, both substantively and temporally. Nor is
the true history of twentieth-century nominations to the Supreme
Court one in which one side has opposed nominees based on the
expected results they would deliver while the other has gone to bat
for judicial restraint on principle. Rather, the true history counts
numerous examples of conservatives and liberals alike opposing
nominees—to whatever extent their power at the time permitted—
on the basis of the divisive issues of the day, be those race, labor
relations, or abortion. Ideological opposition, even ferocious opposition, is not the novelty. What is new, rather, is the spectacle—
driven by live testimony of the nominees, particularly on national
television; the pervasive influence of interest groups; and the meld-
ing of partisan and ideological alignments that were once distinct.
The conservative analysis, in short, offers a useful insight into the
pathologies of the Left, but it accounts for history incompletely
and inaccurately and fails to fully appreciate the Right's own infatuation with modern judicial power.

Liberals offer their own account of the process's decline,
though they generally focus less on the confirmation process itself
than on the goals and ambitions of their opponents in making
nominations in the first place. In the liberal narrative, the process
has deteriorated because of a concerted conservative campaign to
pack the courts with extreme right-wingers in order to accomplish
a great "rollback" of the gains of the civil rights and New Deal

eras. The liberal account, too, has its Golden Age, a period in which Republicans and Democrats alike appointed to the courts jurists committed to protecting civil rights.[26] The Warren Court, for example, had liberals of both parties. Then, in two stages, the Republican Party changed the game. First, as liberal scholar Herman Schwartz writes, Richard Nixon—having pursued his famous "Southern strategy" in 1968 and having made criticism of the Warren Court a major feature of his campaign—"began the process of deliberately restoring the federal judiciary to its traditional conservativism."[27]

This ambition crystallized with the election of Ronald Reagan in 1980, and since that time conservatives have pursued their plan relentlessly. Writes Cass Sunstein, "Since the election of President Reagan, a disciplined, carefully orchestrated, and quite self-conscious effort by high-level Republican officials in the White House and the Senate has radically transformed the federal judiciary." President Reagan and both Presidents Bush have "sought out judicial candidates who would interpret the Constitution and other federal statutes in a way that would promote [their] agenda" to restrict federal power and the rights of the accused, strike down affirmative action programs and campaign finance laws, overturn abortion rights, and breathe new life into constitutional property rights guarantees. While their "most radical goals have yet to be achieved," Sunstein argues, "to a degree that has been insufficiently appreciated and is in some ways barely believable, the contemporary federal courts are fundamentally different from the federal courts of just two decades ago. What was then the center is now the left. What was then the far right is now the center. What was then on the left no longer exists."

Critically, this court-packing effort "has not been limited to Republican presidents." When Bill Clinton occupied the Oval Office, Sunstein says, Republican senators "have been equally single-minded. Showing extraordinarily little respect for presidential prerogatives," they "did a great deal to block [his] judicial nominees."[28]

In contrast, Sunstein describes the Democratic approach to judicial nominations as having "often been passive,"[29] even "astonishingly passive."[30] Indeed, he regards the battle over the courts as "generally one-sided."[31] President Clinton chose, in Ruth Bader Ginsburg and Stephen Breyer, "two centrist justices . . . [who] cannot be seen as ideological counterweights to Justices Antonin Scalia and Clarence Thomas." And Democratic senators have acquiesced to numerous "immoderate" nominees to lower courts. In the current administration, Sunstein concedes, Democrats have been "occasionally more aggressive, blocking a small group that included some of [the president's] most extreme appointees. But the overwhelming majority of President Bush's nominees have been confirmed. At most, Democrats have placed a finger in a dike, with predictably weak results."[32] In short, the liberal account portrays Democratic tactics, even the filibuster, as purely defensive measures designed to fend off, however ineffectually, a concerted attack. The problem lies not in the defense, or in opposing nominees on the basis of their supposedly extreme views, but in the attack itself—that is, in Republicans' having nominated such people in the first place.

As a historical matter, the liberal narrative contains several important insights. First, it is certainly true that presidents preceding Nixon and Reagan, at least in the postwar era, had been decidedly less ideological in their court appointments than conservative presidents are today. Considering Supreme Court nominations, for example, President Harry Truman appointed his friends and political allies.[33] President Dwight Eisenhower named people as liberal as Warren and Brennan, and his conservatives were Harlan and Potter Stewart—who on today's spectrum rank as moderates. Consequently, Nixon did, indeed, mark a break with the past. Tapping Southern and conservative discontent with the Warren Court's de-

segregation decisions and solicitude for the rights of accused criminals, Nixon promised explicitly to name "strict constructionists"
to the bench[34]—a promise that partly conveyed the ambition, reasonable enough, for more serious attention to the Constitution's
text, history, and structure but also shamelessly played to the
South's anxieties about the Court's civil rights jurisprudence.
Nixon's nomination of William H. Rehnquist in 1971 dramatically
expanded the range of acceptable conservatism on the Court,
whose right flank had previously been defined by Harlan and Stewart and, after Nixon's inauguration, by the new chief justice he
appointed, Warren Burger.

Reagan went even further down the path on which Nixon had
set out. Indeed, the Rehnquist experiment hardened over the
course of the Reagan presidency into a kind of orthodoxy—the
modern conservative insistence on some form of originalist jurisprudence as the sole legitimate exercise of judicial power. Particularly during his second term, Reagan did seek a more philosoph-
ically consistent—or ideologically predictable—type of judge, both
for the high court and for the courts of appeals. Liberals, moreover,
correctly observe that at least some of the change in the confirmation process flows from the reaction to Reagan's shift in the
status quo on the nominations themselves; in other words, that the
confirmations became more contentious as increasingly ideological
appointments fueled a heightened perception of threat on the part
of liberals.[35]

But that, in turn, only raises the question of whether the stakes
are now, or ever were, quite as high as the sometimes feverish
imagination of liberals would have it. Indeed, the trouble with the
liberal narrative is that it both pervasively overstates the radicalism
of the conservative judicial project and dramatically understates the
aggressiveness of the response.

For let us be frank: Republicans are not, by and large, talking
about a great rollback of the hard-won gains of the civil rights era—

or even some of the more easily won liberal gains from the modern federal courts. Not any Republicans I know, anyway. Mostly, they contemplate a return in a prospective fashion to a more traditional judicial methodology, one better focused on explicit text and clear history. To be sure, some object to specific precedents, *Roe v. Wade* chief among them. But many conservative judges have shown themselves content to leave what they regard as the sins of the past alone, while resolving to do things differently in the future.

I do not mean to suggest that there exist no radical strains of judicial conservative thought envisioning a more dramatic revision; such strains are real. The "Constitution in Exile" movement, focused on reviving pre-New Deal anti-regulatory jurisprudence, has its adherents.[36] Justice Clarence Thomas flirts with dramatic revisions of federal power and seems to consider no constitutional decision he regards as erroneous as too well-established to revisit.[37] But these no more represent the center of gravity of modern conservative jurisprudence than Justice William O. Douglas represented the center of gravity of the Warren Court. The bite of the conservative judicial movement as a whole—often to the frustration of the Republican base—has proved far less dramatic than its bark.

Indeed, for the past twenty-five years, liberals have described the fate of the Court in apocalyptic terms—as a truck hurtling toward the edge of a cliff and about to plunge into the abyss. Yet somehow, like the turtle who every day walks halfway to the wall, the truck never quite reaches the edge. *Brown* and its many progeny remain orthodoxy, entirely beyond criticism. *Miranda*, we learned a few years ago, is more secure now than it was when it came down in 1966; even Rehnquist managed to make peace with it.[38] The right to privacy is not going anywhere; both Alito and Roberts explicitly testified that they believed the Constitution protects it.[39] The reapportionment cases are not going away, either; the only real question in that area is how much further judicial power in redistricting matters will expand. I do not doubt that, in certain areas—environmental protection most acutely—conservative jurisprudence challenges, even threatens, liberal values.[40] But generally speaking, the stakes seem to me significantly overstated. If *Roe* ever gets overturned, abortion rights advocates will protect reproductive freedoms legislatively.[41] If affirmative action ever becomes inconsistent with reigning conceptions of equal protection, universities and other actors will find creative new ways to cultivate diversity, as, indeed, they did in Texas in response to a court decision that prevented the University of Texas from considering race in admissions.[42] The majority in a democracy tends to find ways of getting what it wants. And the modern Court, for all the hand-wringing of liberal academics and activists, has not closed off major areas of liberal policymaking. In fact, we should ask what exactly liberals have lost as a consequence of the appointment of all these conservative judges—other than the use of the courts as a means for their own judicial policymaking.

Let us be frank on another point as well: It ill-becomes Sunstein, and others, to pretend that nothing very ugly has taken place on the liberal side of this fight. Indeed, to characterize either side's behavior in this struggle as passive or to see the struggle itself as one-sided fundamentally marks one as a combatant within the battle, rather than a sober observer of it. Every time a conservative president makes a Supreme Court nomination—and now, even many times with lower-court nominations—a spasm of rage bursts forth from activists and senators who willingly trumpet gross distortions of the nominee's record, misleading insinuations about his or her character, and sometimes even outright lies. This is not passivity. It was not conservatives but liberals who could not content themselves with defeating Bork's nomination (reasonable enough, in my view) but had to demonize him as well.[43] It was not conservatives but liberals who first permitted the agenda for their confirmation fights to migrate from the senators themselves to the outside interest groups that, to a great extent, now drive the process. It was not conservatives but Democratic senators who demanded that D.C. Circuit nominee Miguel Estrada respond under oath at his hearing to a set of allegations to which nobody was prepared to put his or her name.[44] It was not conservative legal scholars but liberal ones who, working in concert with senators and activists, managed to turn a large swath of the legal academy into a public relations arm of a contemporary political party.[45] I don't mean to suggest here that liberals are more accountable than conservatives for the degradation of the process. Rather, I believe the moral equivalence is exact—indeed that morality itself is the wrong lens through which to view the conflict in the first place. Had roles been reversed, conservatives would have acted the same way; during the Clinton administration, they took some of these innovations and ran with them. That said, it takes intellectual gymnastics to find passivity on the liberal side.

Nor is it correct to describe Clinton's role as a judge-picker as passive. It is true that Clinton never invested the great political energy in his judicial nominations that Bush now devotes to his and that he sought to a greater extent than Bush has to placate the opposition's concerns. But Clinton appointed centrist-leaning liberals to the high court—and to other courts, too—not out of quiescence to Republican demands alone but also as a reflection of his own convictions about the judicial function. Clinton, after all, had run as a centrist, having served for more than a decade as the centrist governor of a Southern state. He never described any aspiration to reconstitute the Warren Court. Ginsburg and Breyer, rather, reflected his governing ideals more or less as Alito and Roberts reflect Bush's. Both presidents used their nominations, as all presidents do, to extend their governing philosophies beyond their terms in office using the life tenure of federal judges.

Finally, if Republican presidents have sought in a systematic fashion to pack the courts with like-minded judges, what on earth is wrong with that? This "disciplined, carefully orchestrated, and quite self-conscious effort" has not been more focused than, say, President Franklin Roosevelt's effort to wrest control of the judiciary from the conservative forces of his day. Packing the courts is what presidents do. Nor has the effort been any kind of a secret. As far back as the 1980 presidential campaign, *New York Times* columnist Anthony Lewis warned, "If Reagan becomes President . . . he would . . . surely—and quite properly—try to pick nominees who share his view of the Court's function and of the country's 'values and morals.'" His model, Lewis wrote, would be then-Associate Justice Rehnquist, whom he characterized as "a judicial ideologue of the right, the most predictable conservative appointed to the Court in fifty years."[46] Since Lewis wrote that column, the American people have had the chance to vote on the program every four years—a total of seven times. And five out of the seven elections since the conspiracy hatched, the populace collectively decided that it does not mind these judges so much that it would prefer giving a Democrat the appointing power. The liberal narrative, in a nutshell, describes much of the broad history of the struggle accurately. But it suffers—as does the conservative version—from selective amnesia. And it all seems predicated on a peculiar fallacy: that it is somehow improper—indeed, both illegitimate and an appropriate subject for resistance—for conservative presidents to govern exactly as they promised, having serially prevailed in national elections.

A fourth approach—call it the Jeremiad school—merits brief mention as well. It puts a pox on both the liberal and conservative houses and sees the change in the process principally in terms of the coarsening of American political culture. Its leading work is law professor Stephen Carter's 1994 book *The Confirmation Mess*, which actually predates the worst Republican abuses during the Clinton administration and all of the Democratic abuses during the current president's term. Carter argues, in essence, that the problem is at its core one of "decency":

> [W]e have reached in our confirmation processes a strange pass at which, once we decide to oppose a nominee, any argument will do. Nobody is interested in playing by a fair set of rules that supersede the cause of the moment; still less do many people seem to care how much right and left have come to resemble each other in the gleeful and reckless distortions that character-ize the efforts to defeat challenged nominations. All that seems to matter is the end result: if the demonized nominee loses, all that has gone before is justified.[47]

For Carter, the modern process is a function of the "media culture"[48] and a general obsession on the part of both broad po-litical movements with getting particular results from the courts. "When a new Justice is selected, what hangs in the balance is nothing so arcane as the correct approach to constitutional inter-pretation," he writes, but "the list of rights to be protected or un-protected, depending on one's preference. The public . . . does not particularly care *how* the nominee will reach her results. The public cares only about what results the nominee will reach. And as long as that is our national attitude about the Supreme Court . . . our battles over the rare vacancies will all too frequently be bloody."[49]

Carter's point here strongly resembles the conservative critique, except that he makes his argument even-handedly: The right be-haves no better than the left. Both sides "alike are ready to sacrifice anybody's reputation, because *our side cannot possibly be allowed to lose!* It is not, however, a war fought in the spirit of Tom Wolfe's fine definition of the right stuff—the uncritical willingness to face danger. It is, rather, a war that demands the uncritical willingness to place others in danger" (emphasis in original).[50] Carter laments the passing of an old, more civilized, way of handling nominations and argues that the system can work that way again "if we surrender the bold and exciting image of the Supreme Court as national policy-maker and recapture in its stead the more mundane and lawyerly image of the Supreme Court as—dare I say it?—a court."[51]

I confess a great deal of sympathy for this approach to the problem. Carter's argument admirably transcends contemporary partisan bickering. Animated by appropriate indignation at the indecency of the modern process, he rightly laments what your average kindergartener (if not your average senator) would recognize as downright meanness. This approach sees, I'm sure correctly, thematic connections between the ferocity of confirmation fights and other signs of greater political polarization. My newspaper's many editorials on judicial nominations contain a similar concern for declining civility and sense of fair play and a similar disgust for the raging partisanship that has overtaken many modern nominations.[52] Indeed, as a normative matter, I do not see how anyone could argue with Carter's call for everyone to respect law and each other more deeply, for it is earnest, worthy, and civilized.

As does much nostalgia, however, it does induce a kind of paralysis. For Americans are not about to surrender a bold image of judicial power; nor are the forces that drive political polarization and partisanship—whatever one believes them to be—likely to yield before plaintive pleading from one law professor (whose colleagues relentlessly drink at the waters of political polarization) and a few editorial pages. Having observed the problem and pleaded for everyone to act more decently, in other words, what, then, does one do? In Carter's case, the answer is plead some more. At day's end, he can scarcely identify a reform that seems promising or much of a strategy for combating the forces he deplores. Indeed, dismissing such suggestions, he actually concedes that "despite all the worry about blood on the floor and smears and sound bites"— worries he has just expounded at book length—"our processes for nominating and confirming Supreme Court Justices . . . are not really broken. . . . The trouble, rather, is in our attitudes." Only if we fundamentally reorient these "can the confirmation process be fixed."[53]

This seems to me an unfortunate fatalism—and a hasty one at that. For the history Carter recounts, which I shall describe in depth later, does not support the notion that the process has decayed in the face of attitudinal shifts alone. Rather, as I shall explain, it has atrophied partly in the face of policy decisions by the Senate to alter its way of doing business—particularly its decision to demand the live testimony of nominees—and the decisions by the executive branch and the judiciary alike to acquiesce in these changes. To be sure, these changes in some sense reflect the broader attitudinal shifts that Carter bewails. But they also represent discrete policy decisions, decisions we ought not to presume irreversible now. The Jeremiad school represents, in my view, the only authentic moral voice speaking on the process; that is, a moral voice that does not ultimately serve the immediate political agenda of the speaker. But it awaits as a solution something akin to the coming of the Messiah. Some of us do not wish to wait that long. At a minimum, the conflict needs management between now and the time when we all learn to get along better and harbor less grandiose visions of the Supreme Court.

CHAPTER 3

■

The
Transformation
of Judicial
Confirmations

In discussing alternative views of the confirmation process's decline, I have surely tipped my hand concerning my own view of the matter, which I will now spell out more explicitly and in greater detail. It seems inescapable to me that the process has changed fundamentally and for the worse. The process now takes dramatically longer at the lower-court level than it used to even quite recently and somewhat longer at the Supreme Court level, too. Senators think nothing of using it, quite overtly, to push nominees to deliver substantive results. And presidents cannot predictably fill key, or even routine, court vacancies without protracted, nasty, and very personal fights. To those political scientists who either doubt the scope of the change or doubt that any change poses real problems, I submit that all of this is new and quite unhealthy.

Consider first the empirical evidence that presidents of both parties now have an objectively harder time getting nominees confirmed to courts than they used to—a point that is somewhat clearer with respect to lower-court nominations than nominations to the high court. Lower-court nominations from Harry Truman's presidency through Jimmy Carter's constitute a stable postwar baseline against which to measure modern developments. According to data compiled by the Congressional Research Service (CRS), between 1945 and 1980 no president saw fewer than 75 percent of his lower-court nominees confirmed, and only Gerald Ford saw fewer than 80 percent of his circuit nominees confirmed. (Seventy-three percent of Ford's circuit nominees won confirmation.)[1] In the eighteen congresses that took place during this period, the average time from nomination to confirmation varied, but the process was always reasonably expeditious. During the Seventy-ninth Congress (1945-1946), it took as little as seventeen days on average for the Senate to confirm district court nominees and twenty days to confirm circuit nominees. In only two congresses did it take more than fifty-one days to confirm the average district judge or fifty-eight days to confirm the average circuit judge. In these congresses—the first of which met between 1959 and 1960 and the second of which met between 1979 and 1980—the Senate took about three months to confirm the average nominee. But these two congresses are clearly aberrational; bracketing both are congresses that acted far more swiftly. In general, the norm was for the Senate to confirm lower-court judges in, if not less than a month, certainly no more than two.[2]

Then something changed. The first six years of the Reagan administration look quite similar to the baseline; judges took between one month and two to go from nomination to final Senate action. But in the 1986 midterm elections Democrats won control of the Senate, and in the 100th Congress—the same Congress that defeated the Bork nomination—the average time for the Senate to consider a nomination skyrocketed to 136 days for district court nominees and 172 days for circuit court nominees. This is roughly twice the time it took in any other prior period in the postwar era. And, critically, while the next Congress did act more swiftly, the figure did not return to what had been normal. Indeed, in the years since the 100th Congress, it has never come back down to the pre-1986 norm.

In fact, with occasional dips—generally during periods of unified government—it has grown steadily worse ever since, particularly for circuit judges. Despite unified Democratic control of the presidency and the Senate between 1993 and 1994, for example, the average time for the Senate to consider a court of appeals judge remained at 102 days. After Republicans took the Senate in 1994, that figure jumped to 194 days in 1995 and 1996. The following Congress, it rose again, to 262 days, and in the last Congress of the Clinton administration, it actually reached 304 days. While that came down to 169 days during the first two years of the current administration, that is still far more than in the first years of the Clinton administration.[3] During the course of the Bush administration through April 7, 2006, it has taken, on average, 394 days to confirm a circuit court judge and 162 days to confirm a district court judge—figures that for technical reasons cannot be compared simply to those for specific Congresses.[4] By some measures, Bush's nominees seem to have moved somewhat more speedily than his predecessor's.[5] According to data compiled by John R. Lott Jr., which are calculated somewhat differently than the CRS figures, however, Bush's nominees have taken longer to confirm than Clinton's.[6] A true comparison will not be possible until the current administration is complete.

Moreover, the confirmation rates for circuit court judges—although not, evidently, for district court judges—are also falling. In keeping with the postwar norms, Carter got 92 percent of his appeals court nominees through the Senate and Reagan got 88 percent. But the first President Bush got 79 percent, Clinton got only 71 percent, and so far George W. Bush has gotten only 74 percent.[7] In both the Clinton and Bush administrations, many nominees have had to be resubmitted to the Senate following non-action over the course of an entire Congress—sometimes more than once.

The difficulty in getting appeals court nominees confirmed is particularly pronounced with respect to appointments to the U.S. Court of Appeals for the D.C. Circuit, the appeals court that serves Washington, D.C., and, therefore, hears a great many challenges to federal regulatory initiatives. Lott points out that during the Carter, Reagan, and first Bush administrations, nominations to the D.C. Circuit took fewer than ninety days on average. That figure has risen even more dramatically during the Clinton and Bush administrations than has the comparable figure for other circuit courts.[8] Indeed, there has not been an uncontroversial nomination to the D.C. Circuit since 1994, when President Clinton named Judge David Tatel to the court during the last period of unified Democratic government. Since then, the Senate has stalled every single nomination. Clinton's nomination of Judge Merrick Garland got held up for more than a year in a dispute with Senator Charles Grassley over how many judgeships there should be on the court. The Senate simply never acted on Clinton's nominations of Washington lawyer Allen Snyder or Elena Kagan, now the dean of the Harvard Law School. During the Bush administration, Democrats in the Senate filibustered Estrada to defeat, stalled for a while on Roberts, filibustered—ultimately unsuccessfully—Janice Rogers Brown, fought half-heartedly over Thomas Griffith, and stalled Brett Kavanaugh for three years. It is simply no longer possible for presidents of either party to place qualified people on the D.C. Circuit within a reasonable period of time.

Lott offers an additional and particularly disturbing indication of decline. He presents data suggesting that "even after accounting for other factors that likely influence speed and success, nominees with stronger academic credentials have a more difficult confirmation process."[9] These data seem to validate the impressionistic sense of some commentators—including myself—that it is the particularly impressive people of both parties who tend to attract opposition.[10] As Judge J. Harvie Wilkinson, who serves on the U.S. Court of Appeals for the Fourth Circuit and was himself the subject of an early (and now tame-seeming) confirmation dispute, put it in a speech, "I worry that we have reached the point . . . where both sides of the aisle consider intellectual distinction a threatening characteristic in a judicial nominee. There could not be a more unfortunate long-term development from the standpoint of the judicial branch."[11]

The general trend at the lower-court level, in short, is that the ability of presidents to win confirmation for their judicial nominees has eroded steadily since the mid-1980s and that this erosion has proceeded apace irrespective of which party controls the Senate or the White House.

One sees the trend less clearly at the Supreme Court level, where senators have always considered the ideology of nominees and where confirmation battles have erupted periodically throughout the twentieth century—and more frequently still during the nineteenth century. Nonetheless, a close look at the statistics reveals much the same effect. According to CRS data, the average Supreme Court nomination between 1945 and 1980 took forty-seven days from the time of the nomination to final Senate action. One took as little time as a single day, and several took only a few. Since 1981, however, the average time has modestly risen to sixty-seven days, and no successful nomination has required less than a month. Particularly in recent years, most have taken between two and three months. With the glare of publicity on each Supreme Court nomination, rare as they are, endless delays of the type that afflict lower-court nominations are not politically sustainable. But the same effect nonetheless shows up, albeit less dramatically; the data show unmistakably that the Senate is taking longer to confirm presidential appointments. In addition, it no longer confirms justices without a roll-call vote, something it did regularly as late as

the Lyndon Johnson administration.[12] The Senate now engineers
the process so as to bring out whatever controversy may exist about
a nominee, rather than assuming a nominee is uncontroversial
unless and until controversy arises on its own.

The most dramatic indicator of increased partisanship and controversy over Supreme Court nominations lies in the sheer number
of transcript pages confirmation hearings now occupy. Michael
Comiskey reports that between 1930 and 1949, hearings averaged
forty-two pages. That jumped to 264 pages between 1950 and 1969,
and to 1,117 pages in the years since 1970. Even the hearings for
five relatively uncontroversial nominees in the modern era averaged 819 pages.[13]

One does not have to buy naively into the notion of a Golden
Age to acknowledge how profoundly the current situation differs
from the norms of the past. Let us return for a moment, by way
of example, to President Roosevelt's 1941 nomination of Chief
Justice Stone—a Republican who had served as attorney general
under President Calvin Coolidge. Stone's elevation from associate
justice produced the polar opposite of the divisive modern confirmation battle—a kind of outpouring of national affection.[14] Indeed, the only senator to speak on the merits of his nomination
on the Senate floor did so in order to apologize for having opposed
Stone's original nomination to the high court in 1925. Said Senator George W. Norris of Nebraska, the last of a small band of
progressives who had voted against Stone,

> When Mr. Stone was appointed an Associate Justice of the
> United States Supreme Court, many years ago, I opposed the
> confirmation of his nomination and voted against it. In the years
> that have passed I became convinced, and am now convinced,
> that in my opposition to the confirmation of his nomination I
> was entirely in error.
>
> I am now about to perform one of the most pleasant duties
> that has ever come to me in my official life when I cast a vote
> in favor of his elevation to the highest judicial office in our land.

I do this because, while it may not affect the country or the Senate, or even Mr. Justice Stone, it is a great satisfaction to me to rectify, in a very small degree, perhaps, the wrong which I did him years ago.[15]

Many aspects of this episode make it seem quaint. Can anyone, for starters, imagine a future Democratic president nominating, say, John Ashcroft to be chief justice or President Bush placing Janet Reno on the high court? Such a move today is unthinkable. Nor could any nominee today be immediately and universally regarded as an excellent choice and garner confirmation without an extended Judiciary Committee investigation; rather, the Senate's acclamation of Stone seems now almost like an abdication. And does anyone think that if Justice Alito provides worthy and independent service on the bench that—choosing a Judiciary Committee Democrat almost at random—Senator Charles Schumer will take the floor to apologize for his vote against the man? The episode seems quaint precisely because the process *has* fundamentally changed—changed, that is, not merely in degree but in quality—in the more than six decades since Stone's elevation.

Stone's example is not an isolated one. As I noted earlier, President Truman's nomination of his replacement, Fred Vinson, went off similarly smoothly. So unthinkable was a fight that President Eisenhower actually installed Earl Warren—the twentieth-century's most fateful jurist—as chief justice using a recess appointment.[16] The action triggered little adverse public reaction (though when employed in modern times for lower-court nominations by Presidents Clinton and Bush it has produced significant friction with the Senate).[17] And Eisenhower did it as well in appointing Justices William Brennan and Potter Stewart.[18] President John F. Kennedy was able to gain Senate approval for his nomination of Justice Byron White within eight days.[19] Even as late as 1975, President Ford was able to win Senate approval for Justice John Paul Stevens in only sixteen days.[20] The list goes on and on. My point is that it is all well and good to observe that the process of both presidential selection and Senate consideration of justices has always contained strong political dimensions. But it seems to me quite an error to conclude from this that things have not fundamentally changed.

This brings me to a second change, harder to quantify and yet no less obvious—that is, that the process has grown uglier, meaner, and rougher than it used to be. I do not want to overstate this point. The nomination of Louis D. Brandeis in 1916 makes even Clarence Thomas's look pleasant. Yet the Brandeis nomination was an exception, while the Thomas nomination took place within a few years of major fights over William Rehnquist's elevation to chief justice and the nominations of Bork and Douglas Ginsburg. Indeed, the pattern is now well established, particularly when conservative presidents try to nominate conservative justices. Everyone warrants major investigation and the closest of questioning. Unless the opposition party deems the nominee as close to its views as it can hope for from the administration—as happened with Ruth Bader Ginsburg and Stephen Breyer—it will fight. Critically, this pattern has been, for the first time, exported from Supreme Court nominations down to the lower-court level. We fight, in other words, more consistently on more nominations to a vastly broader range of judicial appointments.

And we fight dirty. During the protracted brawl over his nomination, Estrada discovered that somebody had gone through his garbage, carefully separating bills and papers from other trash. He was never able to demonstrate that the incident bore any relation to the nomination—as opposed to being, say, an effort at identity theft—and therefore refrained from making any public allegations about it. I venture the modest guess that at no prior time in our recent history would a lower-court nominee have seriously entertained the thought, let alone assumed the possibility more likely than not, that such an incident would be part of an effort to oppose his nomination.[21] Estrada's contemplation of the possibility, given the circumstances of his nomination, was certainly not eccentric. That fact alone encapsulates the extraordinary change in the way the American political system treats nominations.

Yet in noting the change, it is critical to identify it precisely. It is not, as conservatives often claim, a function of the injection of ideology into a process that previously assessed only merit, temperament, and qualifications. Ideology has long been a big part of the consideration of nominations. As political scientist John Anthony Maltese notes, contentious, ideological confirmation battles began not with Bork but with George Washington's failed attempt to name John Rutledge chief justice in 1795, and they have cropped up again and again throughout American history.[22] This point is so clear as a historical matter that it ought not be controversial today. That it requires amplification and justification merely illustrates how emphatic conservatives have been in repeating their own mythology. For brevity's sake, I confine my rebuttal to twentieth-century nominations.

Those for whom the unprecedented nature of the Bork nomination is an article of faith ought to go back and look at the confirmation of Justice Louis Brandeis. Henry J. Abraham, author of the most definitive work to date on the history of Supreme Court nominations, writes, "The Brandeis confirmation battle still ranks as the most bitter and most intensely fought in the history of the Court, and the delay of more than four months after [President Woodrow] Wilson submitted Brandeis's name to the Senate . . . is still a record."[23] Indeed, looking over the transcript of the endless hearings on the nomination, one is compelled to conclude that Bork and Thomas had it easy by comparison. At one level, the Brandeis hearings, which were laced with anti-Semitism, were not an ideological battle so much as a roving effort to find impropriety in the life and work of the man who would become the first Jewish justice. Witness after witness leveled unsubstantiated allegations against him concerning his work on cases or, if they had nothing specific to allege, simply cast aspersions on his character. One testified, for example, that Brandeis was "guilty of infidelity, breach of faith, and unprofessional conduct in connection with one of the greatest cases of this generation."[24] A former attorney general of Massachusetts testified that "his reputation, as it has come to me, is that of a very active, adroit, and successful business lawyer; a man of unbounded audacity; a man, if you wish to go into questions touching integrity—a man, I should say, of duplicity . . . [of] double dealing; a man who works under cover, so that nobody ever knows where he really is or what he is really about."[25]

But the opposition to Brandeis did not flow exclusively, perhaps not even principally, from prejudice. He was widely regarded as a dangerous radical, and though his politics did not arise much in the hearings—which focused generally on digging for dirt on him—numerous institutions and people opposed him at least partly on that basis. Prominent leaders of the organized bar opposed the nomination, as did former president William Howard Taft, who later became chief justice.[26] Thundering that "There is no act of ȯmission or commission of Woodrow Wilson since he was inaugurated President of the United States so utterly indefensible and outrageous as his appointment of Louis D. Brandeis of Boston to the Associate Justiceship of the United States Supreme Court," the Los Angeles Times called Brandeis "a radical of the radicals" and described the nomination as "an obvious appeal by the President for the political support of the Socialists, Gompersites, law-defying labor union bosses, corporation baiters, wreckers of business and all the discontented and dangerous elements of the population." (For good measure, it also pointed out that Brandeis had "line[d] his pockets with gold as a result of his work as a crafty lawyer in sheltering from harm great shoe-machinery trusts," and then "blossomed forth as a special pleader against 'Big Business.' . . .")[27] Somewhat more soberly, the New York Times opined archly that "if Mr. Brandeis is to enter public life, the legislative hall, not the Bench of the Supreme Court, is the proper theatre for the exercise of his abilities." It warned that "The Supreme Court, by its very nature, must be a conservative body" and "to supplant conservatism by radicalism would be to undo the work of John Marshall and strip the Constitution of its defenses."[28] Brandeis was ultimately confirmed on a 47–22 vote, with twenty-seven senators not voting.

There are important differences between the Brandeis nomination and Bork's seven decades later. Unlike Bork, who testified at length at his own hearings, Brandeis never addressed the allegations against him. Nominees did not begin appearing in person before the Judiciary Committee until later, and Brandeis availed himself of no other outlet either. Asked by the New York *Sun* to comment on the charges, he responded: "I have nothing to say about anything, and that goes for all time and to all newspapers, including both the *Sun* and the moon."[29] So while opponents could rail against his supposed radicalism, they had no opportunity to demand that he either arm them with evidence, repudiate his work on behalf of social justice, or promise not to rule in ways they feared. In addition, the Brandeis hearings, needless to say, predated television, so even had the confrontation between the senators and the nominee taken place, it would not have constituted quite the spectacle for the nation to watch as takes place routinely with confirmations today.

The most important difference between the Brandeis nomination and that of Bork, of course, is that in the end, Brandeis won while Bork lost. But this is by no means a moral difference or a principled one. It simply reflects the relative power of two presidents' Senate allies at two different moments in time. And it should not obscure some broad similarities between the two cases—namely, the similar tactics and the frank willingness of opponents in both instances to see ideology as perfectly legitimate grounds for their stand.

The Brandeis hearings are notable in another respect: They

began the opening up of what had previously been a closed and secretive Senate process. Following quickly on the heels of the 1913 ratification of the Seventeenth Amendment, which subjected senators to direct popular election, they were the first public, investigative hearings conducted on a nominee by the Judiciary Committee. The relationship between these two events, John Anthony Maltese persuasively argues, is clear: "With an eye to popular accountability, the Senate voted to open its proceedings on the controversial nominee. Opponents called witnesses whom they hoped would raise doubts about Brandeis's character and judicial temperament. But Brandeis had widespread popular support, and many senators realized that a vote against Brandeis might hurt them at the polls."[30] While interest groups had played a role in prior nominations, the Brandeis nomination marked a significant procedural step toward the modern system: Popularly elected senators had begun investigating nominees with one eye on their constituents.

Progressives did not wait long to return the favor of opposing a president's nominees on purely ideological grounds. In 1930, they bitterly opposed two of President Herbert Hoover's nominees to the high court—one of them successfully. The debates surrounding these nominations are particularly instructive for their modern feel—that is, their focus on the institutional results the court was producing at the time. Maltese perceptively notes that these two scraps once again closely followed a move on the Senate's part toward greater public accountability—in this case, the Senate's decision in 1929 to open floor debates on nominations, which had previously taken place in executive session.[31]

First up was Charles Evans Hughes, whom Hoover nominated to serve as chief justice in early February. Hughes's confirmation took only ten days, but the brevity of the fight actually masks its severity. Hughes had served on the Court before but had stepped down to run for president in 1916 and, in the intervening years, had become a kind of elder statesman. He served as secretary of state for a spell and also as the leading member of the Supreme Court bar, representing big business in a host of cases during an era of great judicial solicitude for its interests. The opposition to Hughes was not monochromatically progressive; as Henry Abraham points out, "Conservative Southerners opposed him because they viewed him as too city-bred, too record-prone to support national versus states' rights when the chips were down."[32] But the floor debate was dominated by progressive anxiety that the man was just too conservative to put on an already-conservative Court. Senator George Norris—the same Senator Norris who would later apologize for his vote against Justice Stone—put it bluntly and eloquently:

> I am aware that it will be said that I should not oppose the confirmation of Mr. Hughes simply because I do not agree with him on these great fundamental issues. I am aware it can be said that those who, like him, stand for great combinations and monopoly have recently been successful by an overwhelming majority in a general election. I realize the force of this argument. It is at least claimed, and I think with some degree of logic, that the people have recently, in a national election, expressed a willingness for the extension of mergers, combinations, and big business, and that the appointment of Mr. Hughes is only one step in carrying out the policy for which the people of the country recently voted.
>
> Nevertheless, I am not willing that this program should be carried out and brought further to its ultimate fruition by any vote of mine.[33]

Senator William Borah of Idaho expressed similar sentiments:

> Mr. Hughes is a man of high standing, one of the distinguished Americans of this day, a man of wide reputation and of acknowledged ability. . . . I am only concerned with the proposition of placing upon the court as Chief Justice one whose views are known upon these vital and important questions, and whose

views, in my opinion, however sincerely entertained, are not views which ought to be incorporated in and made a permanent part of our legal and economic system.[34]

The opposition to Hughes sounds a lot like what Democratic senators recently argued concerning Roberts and Alito; the arguments, in fact, differ barely a whit. And modern Republicans similarly echo arguments made back then—that is, that merely disagreeing with a nominee does not warrant opposing confirmation. Senator Otis Glenn of Illinois, responding to Borah, noted that

> his position is not one of personal attack upon Mr. Hughes, not one really of attack upon his ability, his experience, or anything of that kind; but after his speech is all read and studied it comes down to the point that the trouble with . . . Mr. Hughes is that upon great questions he is not in accord with the views of the senior Senator from Idaho.

If that is really the standard, Glenn joked,

> One man after another would come up for confirmation, his name sent here from the White House after Mr. Hughes's confirmation had been denied. I can see the senior Senator from Idaho, for whom I entertain such great respect, raising the same objection to each of those men that he raises to Mr. Hughes now. As a final result there could be but one thing happen. The final result would be that the names of those men would have to be withdrawn by the President and the name of the senior Senator from Idaho substituted.[35]

Notwithstanding the opposition, the Senate voted 52–26 to confirm Hughes—who, confounding his critics, proceeded to become one of the great chief justices, remembered largely for having steered the court out of its era of property rights enthusiasm.

The progressives, however, avenged their defeat later that year, when Hoover sought to elevate John J. Parker, a judge on the Fourth Circuit, to the high court. For those who believe that the rejection of the obviously qualified Bork on purely ideological grounds had no precedent in twentieth-century practice, the largely forgotten Parker nomination warrants a close look; it displays almost all of the elements of the later Bork fight. As with Hughes, the progressive case against Parker was entirely ideological in nature. The battle marked the first emergence of the coalition of labor and civil rights advocates who—particularly with the addition of abortion rights activists in the 1980s—have since wielded such a powerful veto over certain conservative nominees. And unlike the Hughes case that had preceded it by only months, here the progressives won; the Senate voted Parker down.[36]

The case against Judge Parker contained two major elements. First, Parker had issued a decision upholding an injunction against efforts to unionize mineworkers in West Virginia who were covered by a "yellow dog" contract—that is, a contract that forbade union membership as a condition of employment.[37] As a consequence, the American Federation of Labor aggressively opposed his confirmation. Testifying before the judiciary subcommittee that considered the matter, AFL President William Green stated, "Our opposition is based upon what we interpret to be his judicial attitude toward these great modern-day economic problems, the problems that arise out of human relations in industry, and we feel that it is not in accord with the highest and best interest of the masses of the people and of the perpetuation of our form of government."[38] Parker and his supporters contended that the judge was merely following Supreme Court precedent.[39] In a public letter, the judge asserted that "I followed the law laid down by the Supreme Court" and insisted that doing so was his duty. "Any other course would result in chaos," he wrote.[40] But this argument served him no better than it does judges today who try to answer in the confirmation process for politically unpopular decisions they deem compelled by precedent. The issue dominated the hearings and the Senate's lengthy floor debate.

The second issue hounding Parker was a speech he had given on race issues ten years earlier, when he was running for the governorship of North Carolina. Ironically, Parker's speech actually appears to have been an effort to keep race *out* of the campaign. Running as a Republican—a party still suspected by many Southern whites then of advocating racial equality—he directed his comments at "the attempt of certain petty Democratic politicians to inject the race issue into every campaign." This, he claimed, was "most reprehensible. I say it deliberately there is no more dangerous or contemptible enemy of the State than men who for personal or political advantage will attempt to kindle the flame of racial prejudice or hatred." The trouble was that Parker's strategy for removing race from the campaign was essentially to forswear black voting rights. "The negro as a class does not desire to enter politics. The Republican Party of North Carolina does not desire him to do so," he said. "The participation of the negro in politics is a source of evil and danger to both races and is not desired by the wise men in either race or by the Republican Party of North Carolina."

The speech led the National Association for the Advancement of Colored People to come out against the nomination. Walter White, then acting secretary of the group, testified that "no man who entertains such ideas of utter disregard of integral parts of the Federal Constitution is fitted to occupy a place on the bench of the United States Supreme Court. . . . If Judge Parker, for political advantage, can flout two amendments to the Federal Constitution to pander to base race prejudice, we respectfully submit that he is not of the caliber which loyal, intelligent Americans have the right to expect of Justices of the Nation's highest court."[41]

Parker, in his letter, dismissed the comments, saying, "I have no prejudice whatever against the colored people and no disposition to deny them any of their rights or privileges under the Constitution and the laws."[42] His subsequent career on the Fourth

Circuit, where he served with distinction for many years after his defeat, seems to bear him out. Indeed, Abraham—who describes Parker's defeat as "all but universally regarded not only as unfair and regrettable but as a genuine blunder"[43]—notes that he went on to write pioneering civil rights decisions.[44] For his part, the NAACP's White described Parker's "decisions on both Negro and labor cases" as "above reproach."[45] But without the benefit of hindsight, the combination of the speech and the "yellow dog" opinion made Parker toxic for the progressives. Borah described him as "committed to principles and propositions to which I am very thoroughly opposed."[46] He insisted that it is not enough that high-court nominees "be men of integrity and of great learning in the law" but that "the widest and broadest and deepest questions of government and governmental policies" constitute legitimate considerations, too. "And, finally," Borah said, "we must weigh his conception of human rights, for we all know that the law takes on something of the heart and soul, as well as the intellect, of those who construe it."[47] Parker went down on a 41–39 vote.

Again, aspects of the Parker and Hughes nominations differ markedly from the modern process. The quality of the debate over Parker and Hughes was extremely high by modern standards. Senators on both sides of the fight were impressively learned in law, and in the absence of television cameras they sought to a far greater extent than modern senators do to persuade each other with their speeches, not to pander to a national audience. Moreover, as with Brandeis, the nominees did not testify personally, though Parker indicated his willingness to do so and did write letters responding to allegations against him.[48] And importantly, because ideological lines did not then track party lines as closely as they now do, the debates were not partisan; key leaders in the fights against these Republican nominees were themselves progressive Republicans. Still, these debates have a decidedly modern feel. One side argued narrowly for confirmation based on qualifications, the other for a broad consideration of the nominee's views.

That pattern continued—although with the ideological lines once again redrawn—following the Court's decision in *Brown* almost two-and-a-half decades later. Eisenhower nominees John Marshall Harlan and Potter Stewart, particularly the latter, both ran into trouble with Southern segregationists and extreme conservatives, who feared they would continue on the Court's path toward desegregation and, in Harlan's case, that he supported international government. Harlan's nomination generated eleven "no" votes and got held up for more than four months. Stewart provoked seventeen negative votes and got held up for a similar period.[49] In both instances, the opposition objected exclusively to their views.

This phase of ideological opposition culminated in 1967 with Lyndon Johnson's nomination of Thurgood Marshall, the nation's first African American justice and the man who had argued *Brown*. Marshall's opponents not only painted him as a dangerous radical but also engaged in a particularly vile set of smears, reminiscent of the attacks on Brandeis a half-century before.[50] Marshall's hearing, to which I shall return later, was a degrading spectacle of racism. The segregationists once again held up the nominee for a while and ultimately mustered eleven votes against him.

Because their objections did not prevail in these cases—indeed, produced only delay and a handful of votes—commentators often ignore the ideological opposition of the segregationists to a string of nominees. That, however, seems to me an intellectual error. The proper analysis is that once again, in a period of great controversy over the Court's work, opponents of the high court's direction reserved the right to oppose nominees who they believed were inadequately committed to changing that direction or who they believed were fervently committed to advancing it.

Ideology also formed a substantial component of the grounds

for the opposition both to President Johnson's attempt to elevate Justice Abe Fortas to chief justice in 1968 and to several of President Nixon's nominees, beginning with his attempt to put Judge Clement Haynsworth on the Court the following year. In both of these cases, other factors confound the effect of ideological anxiety about the nominee. Johnson nominated Fortas, for example, as a lame-duck president, and many senators wished that his successor would name Warren's replacement. In addition, charges of cronyism dogged Fortas, who remained a close friend and adviser of Johnson's, even while on the Court. There were allegations of financial improprieties as well in connection with a speaking fee Fortas had collected—allegations that later ballooned and forced his resignation from the court altogether. That said, frustration with the activism of the Warren Court clearly formed a significant part of the brew that led to Fortas's defeat by filibuster. Responding to news of the nomination, for example, Senator Clifford Hansen of Wyoming declared his opposition not merely because it was "an affront to the American electorate to deny them a voice in selecting a new Chief Justice during this critical election year." Hansen also fretted at length about the "dangerous amount of judicial activism under the Chief Justiceship of Earl Warren during the last 15 years" and expressed his belief that Fortas was a part of the problem: "insofar as Mr. Fortas' decisions can be identified with the Court's activism of the past, I feel compelled to oppose his nomination."[51] At least to some extent, the cronyism and financial charges offered opponents convenient grounds for opposing a nominee they disliked for ideological reasons.

Much the same thing, in reverse, happened in the case of Haynsworth's nomination. It was defeated chiefly because of alleged conflicts of interest in his service as a lower-court judge. The allegations probably would have seemed less significant had Haynsworth's nomination not followed Fortas's so closely; in Henry Abraham's judgment, "the Fortas-Haynsworth connection proved

decisive," leading some senators sympathetic to the nominee's conservative approach to vote against him.[52] Yet again, a big part of
the opposition had more to do with Haynsworth's views than with
his conduct. The liberal coalition that opposed him bore a striking
similarity to the one that had opposed Parker. George Meany, president of the AFL-CIO, testified that his "record is one of insensitivity to the needs and aspirations of workers and to the plight of
unorganized employees" and that "he is instinctively sympathetic
with the problems of employers, including rabidly antiunion
ones."[53] Representatives of the Leadership Conference on Civil
Rights described the nomination as "a deadly blow to the image
of the U.S. Supreme Court" and said that "for Negroes [his judicial
philosophy] means granting their constitutional rights with an eye
dropper at a time when these rights should be flowing like a river
in a thirsty land."[54]

Senators blended the personal and the political in assessing
the nominee as well. Walter Mondale, for example, opposed him
for "his insensitivity to the needs and aspirations of Americans who
have spent the last 50 years struggling for equal rights and the
opportunity to earn a decent living," as well as for the "conduct of
his personal financial affairs."[55] Again, one cannot easily assess how
big a role ideology played, but as with Fortas, Haynsworth did not
receive an evaluation based strictly on Lott's trio of "competence,
propriety, and temperament."

The nomination that succeeded Haynsworth's, that of G. Harrold Carswell, also met with ideological opposition, though again,
the opposition to Carswell had other roots. Many senators regarded
Carswell as mediocre—which he plainly was. But they also feared
he was a racist, and that latter fear, as much as the former, drove
the opposition.[56] And, of course, ideology formed the dominant
factor in the opposition to William Rehnquist, both in his nomination to be associate justice in 1971 and in his elevation to chief
justice in 1986. In the latter instance, other allegations clouded

the nomination: that Rehnquist had opposed *Brown* as a law clerk to Justice Robert Jackson, that he had sought to intimidate minority voters in Arizona, and that he owned properties with restrictive covenants. But these merely supported a larger anxiety: that, as the opponents of Charles Evans Hughes had argued, he was just too conservative to lead the Court.

Put simply, the history conservatives love to cite of senators shunning ideology in considering Supreme Court justices is largely myth. Lott attempts to cabin protracted ideological opposition to nominees prior to Bork as limited to situations that "almost invariably involved race, religion, or serious questions about the competence of the nominee."[57] The argument is unpersuasive. Yes, many of the cases involved race and ethnicity, but as the survey above illustrates, senators by no means confined their objections to potential judges to such questions. In short, as the great constitutional scholar Charles Black Jr. once put it, if the tradition of non-ideological consideration of nominees "exists, [it] exists somewhere else than in recorded history."[58] Indeed, while the process has changed dramatically, we cannot reasonably trace that change to a sudden senatorial interest in the politics, worldview, or ideology of nominees. For a rigorous explanation, we must look elsewhere.

As I have suggested, the proper manner in which to understand the change is not in partisan or political terms at all but, rather, in institutional terms. For while it may have begun as a reaction among Southern conservatives to progressive civil rights jurisprudence, it has persisted and accelerated independently not only of the Court's ideological inclinations but also of whichever broad political movement controls the levers of government. Were one side wearing white hats and the other wearing black hats, we could expect to see the problem growing worse depending on which party or political movement controlled the Senate or the presidency. One can attempt to make this argument for either side. Republi-

cans can argue that the change began in the 1980s when Democrats gained control of the Senate and that the Ginsburg and
Breyer nominations look nothing like the Alito and Roberts nominations. Democrats, on the other hand, can argue that Republican
escalation of the lower-court battles during the Clinton years
eclipses anything that took place before it. In light of the consistent
trajectory of the change and its interruption by neither party's as-
cendancy over a period of two decades, both arguments in all of
their many iterations strike me as weak. To understand why the
shift has taken place, one must go back much further than the
Reagan administration and take a high-altitude look at the relationship between the courts and Congress.

In her recent book on the lower-court appointments process,
political scientist Nancy Scherer identifies "two dramatic events"
during the 1950s and 1960s that have, in her judgment, driven the
subsequent changes:

> First, the political party system changed, from a loosely con-
> nected system of local, patronage-driven organizations into a na-
> tional, policy-driven organization. Second, the federal judiciary
> changed, from a closed institution that adjudicated the property
> and business-oriented claims of corporations into an open insti-
> tution that adjudicated individual rights claims of the disadvan-
> taged. As a result of these two historic changes, politicians—
> presidents, senators, and even candidates for these offices—
> would cease using lower federal court judgeships predominantly
> for *patronage* purposes and instead, in accordance with the de-
> mands of political activists for judges who will be sympathetic to
> their respective causes, would begin to exploit federal judgeships
> as a means to satisfy the activists' *policy* demands.[59]

This admirably concise account seems to me profoundly correct as an analytical matter. It explains, first, the strong tendency
of the political parties in the modern era to identify themselves
with particular modes of judicial decision-making. This tendency

represents a great break from the past, when, for example, the leaders of the opposition to the Hughes and Parker nominations by a Republican president were Republicans themselves. It also focuses on the changed nature of the courts themselves, not by way of condemnation or praise but by way of explaining why American society seems to care so much more today about what its judges believe than it used to. Put briefly, Americans care because judges are deciding more and more issues closer and closer to their lives.

It is this latter point on which I mean to focus, not in order to deemphasize the importance of the shift in the political parties. But that change is so broad that its impact on judicial nominations specifically is necessarily more diffuse and difficult to trace. By contrast, the change in the courts themselves bears an immediate relationship to the shifts in the process, one we can identify with surprising precision. Indeed, we can reasonably describe the decline of the process as an institutional reaction by the Senate to the growth of judicial power that began with the *Brown* decision in 1954.

I should pause a moment to define precisely what I mean by judicial power. Formally, the courts today have the same powers they have always had in the American system since *Marbury v. Madison*: the power to decide "cases and controversies" arising under American law, including the power along the way to review acts of Congress and state legislatures for consistency with the federal Constitution. Aggressive uses of this power, needless to say, long predate *Brown*. The Court that handed down *Dred Scott* was no shrinking violet, after all, nor was the Court that limited the scope of the Civil War amendments, or the *Lochner* or early New Deal courts. In practice, however, judicial power has not been static but ascendant. For the early Court, having expounded its power of judicial review of congressional enactments in *Marbury*, did not use it often, indeed did not strike down another federal law for decades. Even *Dred Scott*, boldly evil though it was, was a single case, not a pattern and practice of judicial aggressiveness. Similarly, the Court's later economic conservatism, however intrusive on democratic government, dealt largely with a single broad area of American life: government regulation of the economic relationship between employers and employees. By contrast, the modern Court has leveraged the same formal authorities into political influence across a far greater range of policy areas. Largely the master of its own jurisdiction, it has seen to it that its jurisdiction has grown to include questions long deemed outside of the judicial function. The courts now intervene in a breathtaking array of democratic decisions and reserve the power to regulate questions of social policy at the core of Americans' sense of autonomy and identity. That change began before *Brown*, but *Brown* crystallized it, and *Roe* later dramatically reinforced it.

Given this history, it should not come as a particular surprise that the critical shift in the confirmation process began with *Brown* and established a new status quo as the Court's aggressiveness increased over the subsequent two decades, culminating in *Roe*. Indeed, the first major watershed was not the Bork nomination; it was, rather, the nomination by President Eisenhower of John Marshall Harlan shortly after the unanimous *Brown* decision came down and while the implementation phase of the case was still pending before the high court. Harlan's nomination marked the first time the Senate sought live testimony from a nominee in order to grill him about his view of specific cases and about his judicial philosophy—a change from which the process has never quite recovered. Few commentators today remember the Harlan nomination, yet in initiating the Senate's unfortunate and sordid history of taking live testimony from judicial nominees on their judicial philosophy, it laid the groundwork for much that is happening today.

For most of American history, the Senate considered Supreme Court nominees without soliciting their input. Politicians considered it an intolerable affront to judicial independence to ask a nominee how he would vote on a matter; to answer any such question was unthinkable. As Abraham Lincoln is reputed to have put it, "[W]e wish for a Chief Justice who will sustain what has been done in regard to emancipation and the legal tenders. We cannot ask a man what he will do, and if we should, and he should answer us, we should despise him for it. Therefore we must take a man whose opinions are known."[60] The simple idea animating this norm was that justices should be independent and anything that smacked of conditioning their appointments on a promise concerning their views eroded that independence—and thus the separation of powers.

In describing the history of nominees' testimony before the Senate Judiciary Committee, commentators generally cite Justice Harlan Fiske Stone's original 1925 nomination and Justice Felix Frankfurter's nomination in 1939 as the first incidents. While literally true, this account tends to mislead. For neither Stone's nor Frankfurter's testimony marked a true break with the traditional inhibitions about probing a nominee's views. Neither hearing bears much resemblance to a modern nomination hearing, during which senators grill the nominees about individual cases or about their judicial philosophies. This tradition, rather, began with Harlan and in direct response to *Brown*.

Stone testified because of a quirk in his nomination unlikely ever to be repeated. Serving as attorney general at the time he was nominated, his department was investigating a senator, Burton Wheeler of Montana, whose lawyer was another senator, Thomas Walsh, also of Montana. The department, under Stone's corrupt predecessor, had filed charges against Wheeler in Montana, alleging that he had represented a private client before government following his election to the Senate; Stone, after agreeing to review the allegations, was contemplating bringing further charges in Washington, D.C. Yet a Senate committee had purported to have exonerated Wheeler, and some senators therefore believed the department to be acting improperly. The hearing, which followed the decision by the full Senate to send the nomination back to the Judiciary Committee, offered Stone an opportunity to set the record straight and defend himself.[61]

As a consequence, the hearing did not focus on what sort of justice Stone would be but entirely on how the department—and Stone personally—had conducted the Wheeler investigation.[62] Grilled for several hours by Walsh, Stone acquitted himself admirably: The *Washington Post* described the result as "a complete and convincing demonstration of Mr. Stone's high purpose and good faith in dealing with the Wheeler case."[63] Stone garnered quick confirmation after the hearing on a 71–6 vote.

Notwithstanding the nonjudicial quality of the interrogation, the Senate's treatment of Stone rubbed people the wrong way. The *Post*, for example, editorialized that the extortionate quality of the incident raised questions about the "fidelity of the Senate itself as a whole." Senator Walsh, the *Post* wrote, "acting in the equivocal capacity of counsel for another Senator under judicial investigation, is virtually saying to the Attorney General: 'I have the power to prevent you from becoming a member of the Supreme Court. If you dare to continue the inquiry before the grand jury into charges against my client I can and shall prevent your confirmation. But if you will violate your oath of office, betray the law and poison the source of justice, I will withdraw my objections and you can become a justice of the Supreme Court.'"[64] Even in its infancy, the hearing presented significant opportunities for mischief.

Frankfurter's hearing responded to a different concern: the notion, advanced by anti-Semites, that the man who would become the second Jewish justice was a Communist.[65] This concern, of course, is ideological, but not in the sense that modern nominations become ideological. Senators did not plumb Frankfurter's attitudes toward individual cases or case areas or even attempt to discuss his approach to adjudication in general. They called him, rather, to reassure themselves that he believed in the American constitutional system in the first place. Frankfurter, in fact, began his testimony by stressing that "I, of course, do not wish to testify in support of my own nomination" and urging that while the committee had an obligation to examine his record, "neither such examination nor the best interests of the Supreme Court will be helped by the personal participation of the nominee himself." As to expressing his views on political or legal questions, he insisted that this would be "improper for a nominee no less than for a member of the Court" and that it would be "not only bad taste but inconsistent with the duties of the office for which I have been nominated for me to attempt to supplement my past record with present declarations."[66] At least as far as discussing jurisprudence, the senators did not pursue the point.

They did, however, seek to clarify the prospective justice's views on communism generally—an effort Frankfurter initially resisted. They asked about his ties to the American Civil Liberties Union, on whose board he served, and its willingness to fight for the rights of Communists.[67] Senator Patrick McCarran of Nevada probed his relationship with the intellectual Harold Laski and asked whether he agreed with Laski's beliefs. If Laski's book "advocates the doctrine of Marxism, would you agree with it?" McCarran asked.

Responded Frankfurter: "Senator, I do not believe you have ever taken an oath to support the Constitution of the United States with fewer reservations than I have or would now, nor do I believe you are more attached to the theories and practices of Americanism than I am. I rest my answer on that statement."

McCarran and Frankfurter later had the following exchange:

MCCARRAN: Doctor, going a little further into your explanation of these matters, do you believe in the Constitution of the United States?

FRANKFURTER: Most assuredly.

MCCARRAN: I am very glad to get that positive answer from you.

FRANKFURTER: I infer that your question does not imply that you had any doubt about it.

At this point, the subcommittee chairman, Matthew Neely of West Virginia, had evidently had enough and brought the matter to a head:

NEELY: [T]he chairman, with great reluctance, propounds one inquiry which he thinks ought to be answered as a matter of justice to you. Some of those who have testified before the committee have, in a very hazy, indefinite way, attempted to create the impression that you are a Communist. Therefore, the Chair asks you the direct question: Are you a Communist, or have you ever been one?

FRANKFURTER: I have never been and I am not now.

MCCARRAN: By that do you mean that you have never been enrolled as a member of the Communist Party?

FRANKFURTER: I mean much more than that. I mean that I have never been enrolled, and have never been qualified to be enrolled, because that does not represent my view of life, nor my view of government.[68]

And with that, the hearing ended and Frankfurter was confirmed without a recorded vote. Nobody had asked how he viewed any specific set of legal issues, nor how he regarded a single precedent of the Court.

Only two other nominees testified at all before *Brown*. Robert Jackson testified for reasons that seem like the mirror image of Stone's case: As attorney general, he had infuriated a senator, Millard Tydings of Maryland, by refusing to prosecute someone Tydings believed had libeled him. Like Stone's, his testimony dealt with what sort of attorney general he had been, not what sort of justice he would be.[69] Frank Murphy voluntarily testified in 1940, just after Frankfurter. No full transcript was made—the nomination being utterly uncontroversial—but brief handwritten minutes suggest that Murphy talked a little more freely about jurisprudence, affirming in the course of defending his record that he believed in "property rights," stating generally that he believed in judicial review "in the proper case" and suggesting this should also apply to states, and disclaiming any belief in "administrative absolutism."[70] Once again, however, none of this was ever tied to any case. To return to Lincoln's formulation, nobody had asked what any of these nominees, as a justice, would do.

All that began changing right after the Supreme Court handed down *Brown*. Prior to the decision, Eisenhower's nomination of Earl Warren had taken place without hearing from the nominee and without much overt discussion of the Court's work at all. Yet by the time Eisenhower sent Harlan's name to the Senate, the world had changed. Southern senators, deeply anxious about the Court's course, wanted reassurance that Harlan would not prove to be a liberal internationalist who did not respect what they euphemistically called state sovereignty. The norm against asking "a man what he will do" was still so strong, and the endeavor of probing a nominee's substantive views on a pending case therefore so disreputable, that they made some effort to mask what they were doing. Instead of focusing on desegregation itself, they attacked Harlan's relationship with a group advocating closer ties with England and his having studied at Oxford, painting him as favoring world government.[71] Indeed, senators grilled Harlan chiefly on the question of whether international treaties such as the United Nations Charter could override domestic law. This issue was broadly related to the South's struggle, since many Southerners feared federal efforts to impose civil rights on their states using treaties rather than the legislative power under the commerce clause—which ultimately became the major lever.[72] Yet the point had somewhat broader resonance than the effort to perpetuate white supremacy; indeed, it had precipitated a considerable movement, not just in the South, for an amendment to the Constitution.[73]

In speaking against the nomination, in fact, Judiciary Committee Chairman James Eastland of Mississippi went so far as to insist that his position had nothing whatsoever to do with desegregation. "I believe that Judge Harlan is an able lawyer," he said. "I think he is too smart and is too able an attorney to accept the views held by a number of Justices as to the effect of the 14th Amendment to the Constitution in segregation matters." Eastland declared that Harlan would be "the ablest lawyer on the Court" and "an improvement over most of the Justices." He insisted that "world government is really the issue in this case."[74]

But as the *Washington Post* editorialized at the time, Eastland and his colleagues "protested too much about not being influenced by the fact that vital segregation cases are before the court."[75] For *Brown* hovered over the entire Harlan hearing. In addition to grilling Harlan at length about the scope of the president's power to make international agreements, an issue that itself had reached the Court with relation to a whites-only cemetery in Iowa,[76] Eastland asked a series of questions that—though he denied it—quite obviously referred to desegregation itself. "Here are some questions that I have been requested by a Member of the Senate to propound," he declared. "Question No. 1: Do you believe the Supreme Court of the United States should change established interpretations of the Constitution to accord with the economic, political, or sociological views of those who from time to time constitute the membership of the Court?"

Harlan understood exactly what Eastland was asking him. "To lay the inquiry bare, as I understand it, you are asking me how I would have voted on the segregation issue?" he asked.

Eastland insisted that segregation "has not anything to do with it," at which point Harlan affirmed that the judge's task is to lay "aside under his oath of office his personal predilections so far as it is possible humanly to do so." Eastland responded, "Of course I knew you would answer it that way." He then went on to ask whether the difficulty of the Constitution's amendment process justifies "the Supreme Court in changing established interpretations" and whether the Constitution denies all legislative power to the courts. While Eastland pretended these questions dealt with abstract matters—indeed, that the questions were not even his—Harlan surely intuited correctly why he asked them. Segregation had everything to do with it.[77]

And, critically, everyone involved understood that Eastland and his colleagues, in asking these questions, meant either to extort concessions or to create a record justifying their votes against Harlan. Harlan had been sufficiently concerned that he had sought the advice of the sitting justices before agreeing to appear. Warren, in a letter, warned him that "if the Committee attempted to probe your mind on legal matters, it would be for a definite purpose and they would not be satisfied with general questions and answers if the matter was opened up at all. Somehow or other, I feel that having been confirmed so recently you will be spared this kind of ordeal."[78] Warren, of course, proved right on the warning, if not on the prediction that Harlan would be spared. For having gotten the nominee to appear and discuss his philosophy, senators immediately began conditioning their votes on the answers they received—or did not receive. Eastland, for example, explained his vote against Harlan, in part, on his having "declined to give his views" on "the legal effect of treaties." The rules had changed. Suddenly, not only did senators reserve the right to "require a nominee to state his views," they reserved the right to vote against him if he refrained, as Harlan had put it, out of concern that "if I undertook to [answer] that would seem to me to constitute the gravest kind of question as to whether I was qualified to sit on that great Court."[79]

The change was not lost on appalled commentators writing at

the time. The *New York Times* editorialized presciently that, "If this line of questioning were to be followed further any candidate for the federal judiciary would have to satisfy the majority of the Senate Judiciary Committee that he was in line with that majority's view." It went on to warn, "The danger of the particular kind of nonsense that has been going on in the Senate Judiciary Committee's hearings is that the separation of powers between the legislative and judicial functions may be broken down."[80] The *Washington Post* described the questions as "highly improper."[81] Harlan himself confided in a letter to Frankfurter that the process was an experience "that should never have [been] associated with a nomination to that great Court."[82] Many nominees since would surely agree.

The segregationists did not wait long to push for substantive answers again. The nomination of William Brennan two years later provoked significantly less Senate opposition, yet the segregationists and the far Right once again quizzed the nominee on his judicial attitudes. Senator Joseph McCarthy, well past his heyday but still capable of abusing almost any Senate process, dominated the hearings—though he did not even serve on the Judiciary Committee. The lone senator to oppose the confirmation of Brennan, whom Eisenhower had installed with a recess appointment, he demanded to know whether "you consider communism merely as a political party or do you consider it as a conspiracy to overthrow this country?" Brennan repeatedly declined to answer various versions of this question, citing cases that might come before him, though he ultimately indicated that he did regard communism as a conspiracy.[83] McCarthy also grilled Brennan on speeches he had given in which he had criticized the excesses of anti-communist investigative efforts.[84] Throughout the hearing, Brennan bobbed and weaved and, at times, he outright pandered, saying at the outset of his testimony, "Not only do I approve" of such congressional investigative efforts, "but personally, I cannot think of a more vital

function of the Congress than the investigatory function of its com-
mittees, and I can't think of a more important or vital objective of
any committee investigation than that of rooting out subversives in
Government."[85] As Brennan biographer Kim Isaac Eisler delicately
put it, "Brennan's performance [was] anything but courageous."[86]

While Eastland did not ultimately oppose Brennan, he did
follow up on his questioning of Harlan with a series of seemingly
abstract legal questions that clearly referred to *Brown*. "It is an
elemental principle, is it not, of constitutional law that an amendment to the Constitution has a fixed, definite meaning when it is
adopted and that that meaning does not change at a later time?"
he asked. Today, such a question might refer to the debate over
whether the Eighth Amendment's meaning is fixed in time or
evolves; in 1957, it clearly referred to the segregationists' contention that the high court had changed the meaning of the Fourteenth Amendment in *Brown*. Brennan declined to answer, though
after a back-and-forth, he stated that the Constitution's meaning
should be determined with reference to its explicit texts and precedents. Eastland then tried to pin Brennan down on what sorts of
materials, other than judicial opinions, a judge might cite as legal
authority. "You don't think then that a college professor when the
current theories of psychology and sociology change that that
changes the Constitution of the United States; do you?"[87] This,
again, undoubtedly refers to *Brown*, which cited academic studies
showing the impact of segregation on black self-esteem.[88]

The Senate, in short, went easy on Brennan—a decision his
career on the bench surely gave some members cause to regret.
But it did so under the new rules, not the old. Beneath an all-but-
transparent mask of asking only abstract questions of legal philosophy, Eastland had reserved the right to probe the nominee's philosophy and attitudes toward cases.

Indeed, in the wake of Harlan's nomination, senators did not
immediately push every nominee to bare his soul. The shift took

place gradually. The testimony in 1957 of Charles Whittaker, who served a brief stint on the high court, occupies only three pages of transcript and focuses quaintly on his humble origins.[89] Byron White's testimony in 1962 scarcely takes up more space—not even five pages of pleasantries with senators too wowed by the former football great to demand an accounting of his likely votes.[90] Arthur J. Goldberg, later the same year, engaged in some colloquies with Senator Sam Ervin—the pompous North Carolinian segregationist and former judge who imagined himself a great constitutional scholar and later won a measure of liberal admiration for leading the Watergate hearings—on what were by then platitudes regarding judicial philosophy.[91]

Senators showed more aggressiveness with respect to Abe Fortas's 1965 nomination as associate justice, which took place in the midst of the Warren Court's revolution in criminal procedure and reapportionment. Fortas engaged in a discussion of crime with Senator John McClellan of Arkansas.[92] Senator Hiram Fong of Hawaii pushed him to address the rather parochial question of whether the Court's reapportionment cases could ultimately deprive small states of their senators. Fortas, after initially refusing to give an answer, actually tipped his hand as to how he would rule— perhaps flummoxed by the stupidity of the question—saying it was "sort of inconceivable" that the cases could be read to override the Constitution's explicit grant of two senators to each state.[93] But if the committee members sometimes behaved gently, they always preserved the foundations of their new rules of play. They invited every nominee to testify, and all of them came.

The mask the segregationists sometimes donned of genteel questioning about general judicial attitude and qualifications came off when necessary—as early as when Eisenhower nominated Potter Stewart, whom he also installed using a recess appointment. At Stewart's hearing, committee members did not satisfy themselves with beating around the bush, though they did quite a bit of that, too. They pushed Stewart, for example, on whether he was going to be a "creative judge";[94] whether he believed in *stare decisis*—in the context of the long-standing doctrine of "separate but equal"; whether he believed that the Constitution and its amendments still meant what they had when adopted;[95] and whether he believed in citing academic literature in judicial opinions.[96] They also, however, asked him repeatedly about *Brown* itself. Senator McClellan put it most directly. "I want to know, and . . . I think all people in this country now are entitled to know of any nominee for chief justice or for associate justice of the Supreme Court of the United States," he said. "Do you agree with the premise used, the reasoning and logic applied, or the lack of application of either or both as the case may be, and the philosophy expressed by the Supreme Court in arriving at its decision in the case of *Brown v. Board of Education* on May 7, 1954?"[97]

McClellan's question provoked a significant response both on and off the committee. Senator Thomas Hennings Jr. of Missouri insisted that he did "not think it proper to inquire of a nominee for this court or any other his opinion as to any of the decisions or the reasoning upon decisions which have heretofore be[en] handed down by that court." He introduced a point of order seeking to restrict such questioning, a point that Senator Eastland, the committee chairman, overruled. Eastland ruled that any senator could ask such questions and that he would respect the nominee's demurral if the nominee deemed the questions improper.[98] The *Washington Post* once again called the questioning "obviously improper" and ventured the suggestion that "Justice Stewart might well have refused to testify at all about any opinion which the Court has rendered."[99] But Stewart took a different course. While he guarded his answers carefully, citing the fact that *Brown*'s progeny were pending before the Court, he also became the first nominee to substantively engage with committee members in their questioning on the merits of a particular decision. He did not entirely refuse to answer McClellan's question. Rather, after a lengthy back-and-forth among committee members as to the question's propriety, the two had the following exchange:

> STEWART: Senator McClellan, the way that question is phrased I cannot conscientiously give you a simple "yes" or simple "no" answer.
>
> MCCLELLAN: Give me an unsimple one with qualifications.
>
>   *   *   *
>
> STEWART: Let me say this so there will be no misunderstanding with this thought in mind. I would not like you to vote for me for the top position that I am dedicated to because I am for overturning that decision, because I am not. I have no prejudgment against that decision.
>
> MCCLELLAN: Is that the only answer you feel you can give?
>
> STEWART: That is not the only one but I am sure, in other words, if I had more time I could say more.
>
> MCCLELLAN: That is as far as you then desire to go in undertaking the answer.
>
> STEWART: That is as far as I feel I can go.[100]

McClellan did not vote for him. And along the way, he and his colleagues had torn down another vestige of the old rules. They no longer even bothered to pretend they were talking about anything other than the Court's specific results.

In the years that followed, judicial power of a generally progressive variety only increased. By the time Lyndon Johnson nominated Thurgood Marshall in 1967, the Warren Court had not only moved decisively on desegregation, it had also initiated its revolution in criminal procedure and rewritten the rules of reapportionment. The Marshall hearings reflect this dramatic increase in the profile of the judiciary, already evident in some of the anxious—though always polite—questioning of Fortas two years earlier. There was, quite simply, a great deal more to talk about than when Stewart and Harlan had come before the committee.

The questioning of Marshall was not always polite—far from it. Indeed, as Henry Abraham aptly put it, the segregationists "had recognized the inevitability of a black appointment for some time, but they were not about to accept it without a battle."[101] The Marshall hearings, therefore, began the tradition of rude and belligerently ideological questioning that has recurred in controversial nominations ever since; its tone, indeed, is reminiscent of the Brandeis hearings a half-century earlier. Unlike Brandeis, however, Marshall did not have the option of declining to engage with the bigots who opposed him. They got to ask him questions and he, if he wished to win confirmation, had to answer them and show respect for an institution and a process that were working hard to render themselves unworthy of respect. The result was a degrading spectacle of the vestiges of public racism picking at a man who surely ranks as one of the great American figures of the twentieth century.

"Are you prejudiced against white people in the South?" Eastland asked him at one point. "Not at all," Marshall answered. "[M]ost of my practice, of course, was in the South and I don't know, with the possible exception of one person, that I was against in the South, that I have any feelings about them."[102]

Senator Strom Thurmond bombarded the nominee with nearly seventy questions, most of them on picayune matters of the legislative history of the Thirteenth and Fourteenth Amendments, in an apparent effort to paint Marshall as ignorant—a kind of confirmation-process version of the just-banned literacy tests for voting. "Do you know who drafted the 13th amendment to the U.S. Constitution?" ("No, sir; I don't remember. I have looked it up time after time but I just don't remember.") "Why do you think the framer said that if the privileges and immunities clause of the 14th amendment had been in the original Constitution the war of

1860–65 could not have occurred?" ("I don't have the slightest idea.") "From what provision existing before 1866 was the due process clause of the 14th Amendment copied, and what was the purpose of copying it?" ("I don't know.") At one point Thurmond asked, "What constitutional difficulties did Representative John Bingham of Ohio see, or what difficulties do you see, in congressional enforcement of the privileges and immunities clause of article IV, section 2, through the necessary and proper clause of article I, section 8?" Marshall said he didn't understand the question. Thurmond read it back verbatim. Senator Ted Kennedy asked for "further clarification of the question, because I really am confused as to what actually you are driving at." Thurmond responded that the question is perfectly plain "if you know the answer. . . . It is just a question of whether you know the answer."[103]

The degrading atmospherics aside, the Marshall hearings also included a substantial escalation of the senators' substantive questioning of the nominee. McClellan and Ervin's demands for satisfaction concerning *Miranda*, which had come down the previous year, take up dozens of transcript pages.[104] Ervin also demanded that Marshall address the Court's opinions upholding the Voting Rights Act and applying it to literacy tests.[105] He attacked Marshall's vote on the Second Circuit—joining an opinion of the legendary Judge Henry Friendly—to insist that the Sixth Amendment required that counsel for an accused murderer be present at an eyewitness identification of the suspect.[106]

And crucially, in posing questions to Marshall, senators made it abundantly clear that their votes depended on the answers he gave. McClellan, after trying repeatedly to force Marshall to give his views on *Miranda*, declared,

> I must say to you that this leaves me without the necessary information I need affirmatively to consent to your appointment. I need it. You have the background, you have the training, and you have the ability. But I do not care who it is that comes before

this committee hereafter for the Supreme Court; I am going to try to find out something about their philosophy and not take the chances I have taken in the past. I mean that. This is a fundamental principle and an issue here that I think I have a grave duty to perform. I have asked these questions in all good faith. I thank you for your attention. I regret I have not been able to get an answer that would disclose to me your viewpoint on these vital issues.[107]

Senator Ervin later exclaimed in frustration at his inability to get Marshall's views, "How can this committee, or how can the Senate perform its duty and ascertain what your constitutional or judicial philosophy is without ascertaining what you think about the Constitution?" Marshall ventured the modest suggestion that Ervin might read his judicial opinions, to which Ervin barked that he did not have time.[108]

Ironically, in their aggressive questioning of the liberal Marshall, Ervin and McClellan set the table for Democratic Senators Schumer and Kennedy's questioning of conservative nominees Alito and Roberts. Suddenly, the nominee bore the obligation of convincing the Senate he warranted confirmation—not merely on the strength of his career but also based on the substance of his views. No question was out of bounds. If the nominee felt ethically barred from addressing certain questions—and Marshall gave away nothing in a grueling and very admirable performance—that was his problem. Anything he said, or refused to say, could and would be used against him.

The segregationists were not the only senators who failed to appreciate the precedent they were setting for future nominees. Their questions appalled the liberals of their day, including some who—in the fullness of time—would go on to adopt their questioning tactics. At Marshall's hearing, Senator Kennedy piously insisted that members of the committee "are challenged to ascertain the qualifications and the training and the experience and the judgment of a nominee, and . . . it is not our responsibility to test out the nominee's particular philosophy, whether we agree or disagree. . . ."[109]

How very quickly things changed.

In 1969, Richard Nixon took office and within his first term had nominated six individuals to the high court—four of whom ultimately won Senate approval. Within those four years, liberals engaged in a historic flip-flop, essentially adopting the insistence of the segregationists—by now, the former segregationists—on the legitimacy of probing questioning concerning judicial philosophy. They did this, the record makes abundantly clear, quite consciously, and for a simple reason: They now had a lot to protect in the aggressive liberalism of the Warren Court. As Stephen Carter aptly put it, "In one of those curious American political inversions, it is now liberals who profess to believe what . . . they [then] termed a gross violation of the separation of powers."[110]

The shift began with Haynsworth's nomination, which took place a scant two years after Marshall's. While allegations of financial impropriety dominated the Haynsworth hearings, senators discussed the nominee's judicial philosophy as well—and for the first time, liberals directly probed the nominee's attitude toward specific cases. Senator Philip Hart of Michigan asked Haynsworth whether he agreed with Earl Warren's rejection of the "separate but equal" doctrine (he did) and whether he had a problem with the Court's insistence that the state must give indigent defendants counsel ("Senator, we have upheld that right again and again in my court."). The exchange provoked Senator Ervin to interject: "I am glad at long last the Senator from Michigan agrees with me that a Senator has a right to ascertain the view of a nominee for the Supreme Court. . . . I am glad to have a convert to my philosophy. However, I never did get one of the previous nominees to ever reveal any of his political or constitutional philosophy. And I was told at the time that it was highly improper for me to seek to ascertain it." Hart responded that he "was trying to figure out a device that would enable me not to backtrack on the position I have taken earlier, and nonetheless . . . find out if we were asked to consent to the nomination of a man who thought that the direction of the Supreme Court under Earl Warren should be reversed or modified." Haynsworth sagely interjected in the middle of Hart's speech that this "is very hard to do." Hart, to complete his conversion, declared that "on [the] answer [to this question] hinges, I suspect, my vote."[111]

By the time of Rehnquist's nomination in 1971, a nomination liberals contested largely on ideological grounds, liberal senators, having gone in for a dime with Haynsworth, went in for the rest of the dollar. Rehnquist himself had an awkward history on the question of the Senate's probing of nominees, having written a law review article in 1959 egging the segregationists on, indeed, criticizing them for not inquiring aggressively into Charles Whittaker's judicial philosophy.[112] He was, therefore, badly situated to object to the legitimacy of his own interrogation and, to his credit, he did not try. Rather, he stood by his writing, saying to laughter in the hearing room that he had "no reservation at all about what I said from the point of view of the Senate. I think I did not fully appreciate the difficulty of the position that the nominee is in."[113] Throughout the hearings, he tried to answer questions to the extent that he could. Kennedy interrogated him on the constitutionality of congressional efforts to end the Vietnam War,[114] on prior restraints on speech,[115] on wiretapping,[116] on the right to counsel, on reapportionment, and on public accommodations laws.[117] Senator Birch Bayh of Indiana pushed him for proof of his commitment to the Bill of Rights,[118] on women's rights under the Fourteenth Amendment,[119] and—in a sign of things to come—on the right to privacy.[120] Other senators asked how he balanced individual rights against property rights,[121] about his view of reasonableness under the Fourth Amendment,[122] and about a range of additional issues. No senator seems to have publicly taken the position that such questioning was as illegitimate in defense of the Warren Court as it had been over the previous fifteen years in attacking it. The segregationists had managed to normalize it.

A similar change took place over roughly the same period with lower-court nominations, though much more slowly. Curiously, live testimony by lower-court judges before the Senate Judiciary Committee became routine significantly earlier than did testimony by potential Supreme Court justices. And the occasional hearing became contentious quite early. Normally, however, nominees would show up and give the most basic biographical information about themselves and the committee would waive the matter to the full Senate for a vote. Some transcripts of such hearings were published.[123] Many more—like that of Frank Murphy's nomination to the Supreme Court in 1940—were so perfunctory that transcripts were either never published or, I suspect, never prepared at all. Judicial nomination hearings seem to have become far more numerous in the mid-twentieth century.[124] In the years after *Brown*, questioning clearly grew more political, though erratically so. In the late 1950s, for example, committee members forced some would-be judges to take an oath to "support and defend the provisions of Article I, Section 1, of the Constitution that 'all legislative powers herein granted shall be vested in a Congress of the United States'" and "not to participate knowingly in any decision designed to alter the meaning of the Constitution or any law passed by the Congress and adopted under the Constitution."[125] This particular pressure tactic did not last. And in general, the decline of the lower-court process lagged considerably behind the erosion in the norms for Supreme Court confirmation questioning. Still, the change is dramatic over time. By the second half of the Reagan administration, there were notable and explicitly ideological battles over circuit court nominations. These were quaint by current standards. Democrats, for example, demanded recorded votes on some nominees, to enable their votes against them to be preserved for posterity. They defeated district court nominee Jeff Sessions — now a senator from Alabama — in the Judiciary Committee, where they also buried Bernard Siegan, a nominee to the U.S. Court of Appeals for the Ninth Circuit. And they mounted a significant floor fight against Daniel Manion's nomination to the Seventh Circuit; Manion's ultimate confirmation required a tie-breaking vote by then-Vice President George H.W. Bush.[126] But if these fights seem tame by today's standards, their import, in retrospect is quite clear. The lower-court confirmation process was beginning to catch up with where the Supreme Court confirmation process had already been for some time.

Indeed, by the second term of the Reagan administration — the era of Rehnquist's elevation in 1986 and the Bork nomination in 1987 — the norm of smooth confirmations and against forcing nominees to forecast their future behavior had all but evaporated. Concerning the questioning of Supreme Court nominees, it had evolved into a norm of mutual hypocrisy — as it has remained ever since. Liberals now reserve the right to question conservative nominees aggressively and to fret about judicial independence when conservatives question liberal nominees similarly; conservatives do precisely the same with respect to liberals. The flip-flopping compounds over successive nominations. Thus, at Ruth Bader Ginsburg's hearing, when Senator Orrin Hatch pushed the nominee to answer questions about the constitutionality of the death penalty, then-committee Chairman Joseph Biden triumphantly read Hatch his own statement from David Souter's nomination three years earlier, in which he had encouraged Souter to refuse to address such questions.[127] Yet during Roberts's hearings, Biden attacked Roberts's refusal to address questions about abortion and, indeed, tried to get Roberts to address the substance of a series of questions Ginsburg had addressed.[128] And Hatch once again defended the prerogative of the nominee to decline to address questions.[129]

Since both parties practice this new norm, we ought to ignore both sides' rhetoric in gleaning the new institutional position of the Senate. Put simply, the position of the Senate over time—despite whatever any individual senator may say in any given situation—is that any senator is entitled to ask any nominee any question and hold either his answer or his refusal to answer against him if the senator so chooses.

Even on its own, this new institutional posture would probably create a substantial tension in the relationship between the three branches of government over nominations of any controversy. The Senate, after all, is demanding precisely what the nominee cannot give, often motivated by the correct suspicion that his or her attitudes would, if known, preclude confirmation or, at least, engender substantial opposition. But the new senatorial attitude did not occur in a vacuum. It took place against the backdrop of generally increasing partisan polarization. As noted earlier, the opposition to Hughes and Parker, both named by a Republican president, was led by Republicans. The ideological divide and the partisan split of the day were all but unrelated to one another, as one senator even noted on the floor during the Hughes debate.[130] The segregationist opposition to liberal nominees, similarly, was largely a spat within the Democratic Party, though the occasional right-wing Republican from elsewhere in the country took part. By the time of the Bork nomination, by contrast, the parties had largely aligned themselves across the central divisions of the day. So the opposition to Bork, a Republican appointee, was very largely Democratic—only six of the fifty-eight senators voting against him were Republicans, while only two of the forty-two senators voting for him were Democrats. That trend has only hardened since. Only one Republican voted against Alito, and only four Democrats voted for him.

Then, of course, there is television. When the segregationists roasted Potter Stewart and Thurgood Marshall, they did so without the public watching closely. By the time Bork faced the committee, the public could tune in live, cameras having been introduced during Sandra Day O'Connor's hearings in 1981. I have trouble objecting to cameras as a matter of principle; why should the public not have access to these important government deliberations? Yet reading over the history of confirmation hearings, one must conclude that they have had terrible consequences for the quality of senatorial debate on nominations, and probably on other subjects as well.

The coarsening of senatorial debate, to be sure, began long before the advent of C-SPAN. By the time of the Harlan and Stewart nominations, in fact, the floor debates had degraded noticeably from their quality during the Parker and Hughes deliberations. Relatively few senators seemed conversant in case law; a great many more of them were simply posturing. Perhaps, therefore, we should trace the decline in the quality of Senate deliberations to the Senate's having become a less elite institution as time took it further from the Seventeenth Amendment. Yet, at least in the confirmation process, it was cameras that iced the cake. By the time of the Bork nomination, senators used the hearings—and the debate as well—to talk not to each other but to the public, to their supporters, and to the interest groups. Gone were the days when a senator might actually give a floor speech hoping to influence his colleagues' votes.

Indeed, the combination of intense publicity and spectacle, polarized politics, and the elimination of the one norm that had inhibited senators in their interactions with a nominee has proved a bed of dry tinder. And driving it all, making the tinder drier by the day, is the ever-growing scope of judicial authority; that is, the investment that all sides in American politics have in the courts and what they hope to get from them.

The liberal investment in the courts, by the time of the Bork nomination, had dramatically escalated even beyond where it had been when Nixon was naming judges—largely as a consequence of *Roe v. Wade* and its progeny. Since then, the stakes for both sides have only grown, as the high court has dallied with gay rights, the revival of federalism, and an aggressive approach to property rights. The courts today have their hands in a mind-boggling array of political decisions in which they would not have involved themselves in the past: the conduct of war, the consideration of race in university admissions policies and the drawing of congressional districts, the display of religious symbols in public, medical marijuana, the right to die, and school vouchers, to name only a few. The list is so long that one cannot begin it without developing a certain anxiety about how much power over our lives we have delegated to unelected judges.

This is, I suppose, what Stephen Carter means when he says that the solution to our judicial nominations battles is to "surrender the bold and exciting image of the Supreme Court as national policy-maker and recapture in its stead the more mundane and lawyerly image of the Supreme Court as . . . a court."[131] Yet Carter prescribes a drug that does not exist. For no light switch can simply turn off the American love affair with judicial power. In the common political parlance, liberals love judicial power and conservatives hate it. The liberal infatuation with the judiciary has eroded a bit in recent years, particularly after *Bush v. Gore*, but the rule still holds generally true. Liberal mythology continues to sport a heroic vision of the courts as protectors of individual rights from oppressive majorities, while conservatives still purport to seek modesty and restraint from judges.

The reality, as I have suggested, is far more complicated. For judicial power today actually flows from a fairly broad political consensus that we need it; the only question contemporary political movements seriously contest is the ends to which that power ought to be deployed. Liberals, to caricature the broad ambitions of the movement, seek a judiciary that energetically protects personal liberties, particularly sexual liberties, and limits the power of the executive branch at both the state and federal levels. They applaud judicial power to protect the rights of accused criminals and to compel the inclusion in society of historically marginalized groups. They want judges to read the First Amendment to protect soft porn but not soft money. Conservatives, meanwhile, seek a judiciary that aggressively polices the boundaries of federal power and energetically protects property rights, and sometimes gun rights, too. They want judges to restrain race-consciousness on the part of government, whether in state redistricting or in university admissions. They want judges who will read the First Amendment as having less to say in defense of soft porn than in defense of soft money.

One can argue all day about which vision keeps better faith with the Founders, the text of the Constitution, morality, modernity, or just plain old common sense. But neither broad vision, in my view, evinces much judicial modesty or abstention. There are, of course, individual judges of both parties who take a strong stand in principle for a small judicial footprint and who demonstrate a willingness to give up their favored areas of judicial energy in order to get it. Some justices, such as Frankfurter, even put their money where their mouth was while on the Supreme Court. But they are exceptions. Indeed, deference is not a principle with much of a constituency, except a rhetorical one. The most deferential justice of recent times, Byron White, died without a particular following in either party. Both Roberts and Alito cast themselves at their hearings as seeking a modest judiciary. I have no reason to believe either insincere. I do believe, however, that to whatever extent they actually put this into practice, they will alienate the political movement that pushed for them and gain themselves no friends on the Left. For they will be practicing a kind of judging to which our political system somehow aspires without actually wanting.

In short, the dam may have broken during Reagan's second term but it had been rotting for many years before. Why did it finally break then? Here, the liberal and conservative narratives converge and are quite helpful: Reagan forced the issue by appointing people to the bench who—it was reasonable to imagine—were genuinely committed to using judicial power very differently from the way liberals wanted to see it used. Bork, after all, had a long record. It probably was not reasonable to ask Democrats and moderate Republicans to support a man who had described the incipient Civil Rights Act of 1964 as containing a "principle of unsurpassed ugliness."[132] At the appellate court level, it suddenly no longer made sense to vote for people who either believed things diametrically opposed to one's own convictions or who refused to say what they believed. Against a backdrop of ever-rising judicial power, having demolished and never reestablished the key restraint, and with a conservative president actively seeking to make a dramatically different type of appointment to the bench, what was really left to hold back the flood?

One can try to assess this shift in partisan terms. One can blame liberals for believing too strongly in judicial power or conservatives for not being truer to their principled objections to it. One can blame Reagan for appointing judges who reflected his philosophy or liberals for opposing them. One can blame conservatives—though not Republicans—for beginning the tradition of grilling nominees, or one can blame liberals for their farcical embrace of that tradition after years of opposing it. But all of this seems to miss the forest for the trees. The relevant point is that the norms of senatorial restraint gave way in the face of bold and consistent assertions of judicial power over time—assertions that while inconsistent in terms of whose partisan or ideological interests they advance are wholly consistent in terms of whose power they aggrandize. That is, the Senate, responding to a sustained claim of power by the courts, decided to mind the gateways more carefully.

And that is probably as it should be. Indeed, at least part of this shift seems inevitable in retrospect. As James Madison put it, the separation of powers, by design, gives "to those who administer each department the necessary constitutional means and personal motives to resist encroachments of the others."[133] The "advice and consent" power the Constitution gives the Senate enables that body to calibrate the aggressiveness of its confirmation process to its sense of threat from the judiciary's exercise of power. It only stands to reason that a sustained broadening of judicial authority over more than fifty years would trigger some degree of recalibration.

What does not seem inevitable is that the Senate would choose to mind the gateways in the specific way that it did, which seems both ineffectual and needlessly tortuous for nominees. One could imagine, instead, blocs of senators, taking their "advice" function seriously, requesting the nominations of particular judges and politely refusing to confirm presidential appointments not chosen from their lists. One could imagine that the questioning of nominees might have evolved into private, staff-level depositions designed to be informative, rather than high-profile, inquisitorial public hearings designed to be spectacular. One could even imagine the Senate leadership, over time, demanding an opportunity for a sort of pre-appointment veto as a condition of a positive vote. While the judiciary's aggressiveness probably necessitated some response, there were many ways the Senate might have emboldened its own role in the appointment of judges. The specific path it took flowed from choices, not from the inexorable logic of the situation.

CHAPTER 4

■

The
Threat to
Independent
Courts

But do these changes pose a real problem? So what, the skeptic
may reasonably ask, if the process has become less genteel, less
pleasant? Isn't that life in the big city? Judicial nominees, after all,
are applying for high-profile jobs in which society invests huge
trust. We cannot remove them or control them once they take their
seats except in the most extreme of circumstances. Why shouldn't
the Senate put them through the wringer first?

This question must be where the rubber hits the road in any
discussion of the process, and all too often its answer is assumed,
rather than addressed. For the unpleasantness of the modern confirmation system alone cannot condemn it. We do not force anyone to become a judge. Nominees know full well that all aspects
of their lives will come under the microscope when they allow the
president to advance their names. However badly that decision

sometimes rebounds against worthy individuals, nobody today lacks for notice of how roughly the system plays. If people still willingly let presidents nominate them, what exactly is the problem? Indeed, identifying the real harms of the process turns out to be tricky.

Many commentators have worried that people simply will not accept judicial appointment at the cost of submitting to a process so awful or, alternatively, that rigorous ideological inquiry disfavors nominees with long paper trails and encourages the appointment of nonentities. To be sure, Senate confirmation raises the potential cost of entry to the judiciary—a cost that already generally includes, for nominees in the private sector, a huge pay cut. It is reasonable to expect that the harder confirmation becomes, the fewer individuals will consider the judicial life an attractive alternative to lucrative private practice.

But the truth is that we simply do not know how many people get dissuaded from accepting judicial appointments out of fear of the process. Some certainly do; incidents have even become public in recent years. The White House let slip, for example, that after his debacle with the Senate during his nomination to the D.C. Circuit, Miguel Estrada refused to be considered for the Supreme Court vacancy that ultimately went to Alito.[1] One can reasonably hypothesize that lots of well-qualified people who value their dignity or who have some blot on their pasts they prefer to keep private—cocaine use, hiring an illegal immigrant, an extramarital affair—might be declining nominations, and that the process thereby harms the quality of the judiciary. But until presidents begin releasing information about who has rebuffed their staffs concerning potential appointments, which hardly seems likely, this point will remain a hypothesis, not a demonstrable effect.

Moreover, presidents hardly lack for well-qualified nominees. If President Bush had to settle for Alito, a fifteen-year veteran of the court of appeals who had served in the solicitor general's office and as a United States attorney, he hardly got cheated—at least in terms of qualifications and general legal expertise. Indeed, there is little evidence that the quality of the judiciary is slipping; to the contrary, it is more professionalized today than ever before. In an interesting examination of justices' reputations over time among polled scholars, Michael Comiskey concludes that the reputations of modern justices are slightly higher on average than those of justices over the course of either the whole twentieth century or the period before the modern nomination process—though his analysis also suggests that we may be getting fewer truly outstanding justices than before.[2] In other words, the legal profession seems to be generating enough qualified lawyers to compensate for however many the confirmation process is scaring off. Whatever long-term threat the modern confirmation process may pose to judicial quality, it has not yet been realized.

A more immediate source of potential damage lies in the imprinting of partisan identifications onto nominees whom we then expect to act as disinterested interpreters of law. This represents, in my view, a cause for genuine concern. Nobody can imagine that Clarence Thomas's experience before the Senate did not firmly teach him, to whatever extent he did not already know, which side he was on.[3] This problem presents itself more acutely in modern times than it did before the nation's ideological and partisan divisions came to be aligned so neatly with one another. Alito went to the court knowing that he got there for no political reason other than that Republicans supported him. While the vote in Roberts's case appeared somewhat more bipartisan, we can say much the same for him; had Democrats had a chance of defeating him, they might well have taken it. While in an ideal world nominees would all put behind them the circumstances surrounding their confirmations and act impartially, this requires in some cases an almost superhuman self-discipline we cannot reasonably expect of real people. A highly politicized appointments process, therefore, risks creating Democratic and Republican caucuses on the courts of precisely the type a society committed to impartial courts cannot afford.

But again, this risk does not appear to have yet been realized in any demonstrable fashion. In general, the courts today do not seem riven by partisan politics. Two members of the Supreme Court's liberal flank, Justices John Paul Stevens and David Souter, received their commissions from Republican presidents, after all. And while ideological divisions exist on most of the courts of appeals, partisan division among judges is not an especially acute problem. Exceptions exist: The U.S. Court of Appeals for the Sixth Circuit has looked in recent years like a partisan battleground. But there is little reason to think that the imprinting effect of the confirmation process on its judges has played much of a role in its deterioration. In any event, an effect of this type on any court would necessarily be subtle and nearly impossible to measure. Judges, after all, do not hand down their opinions while announcing that "I rule on the conservative side because liberal interest groups and senators viciously opposed my nomination." They do not, by and large, violate their judicial oaths to get revenge for confirmation nastiness. To the extent that such calculations affect their work, rather, they surely do so subconsciously. However legitimate the worry—and I believe it very legitimate—the concern about partisan imprinting is too speculative a basis on which to condemn our modern system for confirming judges.

So, too, is the worry that lower-court judges will pull their punches on polarizing legal questions out of fear of hurting the chances the Senate will consent to their elevation some time down the road. Again, the concern is certainly plausible: Why should a district judge stick her neck out and follow precedent in a politically dicey case that riles public passions and, thereby, render herself controversial? Why not choose the more popular side and let the appeals court take the heat for reversing? I am sure that such pressures exist for judges with bright futures, if only subconsciously;

indeed, I would be surprised if some were not influenced by them. Yet the effect is, once again, impossible to demonstrate.

The danger that seems to me both tangible and demonstrable is the one, quoted earlier, that the *New York Times* articulated in its editorial back when Harlan first testified before the Judiciary Committee: "If this line of questioning were to be followed further any candidate for the federal judiciary would have to satisfy the majority of the Senate Judiciary Committee that he was in line with that majority's view. . . . The danger of the particular kind of nonsense that has been going on in the Senate Judiciary Committee's hearings is that the separation of powers between the legislative and judicial functions may be broken down."[4] At least the first half of this anguished prediction of five decades ago has clearly come true. And we should, at a minimum, worry that the rest will follow. That is, the new rules for confirmations pose substantial challenges for the maintenance of independent courts over time.

These challenges have both an immediate and a longer-term — and admittedly more speculative—dimension. The immediate concern is the impossible position in which the Senate places nominees nowadays. Consider, once again, the most recent high-court nominations. It seems inarguable that had Democrats possessed a majority in the Senate, they would have voted Alito down and would not have given Roberts such smooth sailing. This point works the other way, too. Based on their efforts to stop Clinton's nominees to the lower courts, we can fully expect Republicans to oppose qualified liberal nominees to the high court in the future — their current rhetoric notwithstanding. Nor do Ginsburg and Beyer's cases offer much reassurance. Republicans, to be sure, voted for them both in large numbers. But they did so less out of deference to the president's choices than because their leadership deemed them the most attractive appointees they could reasonably hope to get from Clinton. And this took place before they then gained control of the chamber and dramatically escalated the wars over lower-court judges.[5] In any event, whatever one makes of these and Roberts's case, Alito's gives the game away. We have arrived in the era of party-line consideration of nominees, an era in which the nominee has to satisfy the majority of the Judiciary Committee on substantive questions.

During periods of unified government, a party-line vote merely diminishes the strength of a nominee's national affirmation. Alito, after all, did get confirmed. But what if the majority of the Judiciary Committee does not share the president's ambitions for the courts? By happenstance, this situation has not arisen at the Supreme Court level since Thomas's nomination in 1991, but it surely will again. When it does, the president and the nominee will both face an unenviable situation. The president (of whichever party) will have to choose either to satisfy the opposing party by naming someone as close to its members' liking as they can reasonably hope to expect—someone akin to Ginsburg or Breyer from the Democratic side or to O'Connor or Justice Anthony M. Kennedy from the Republican side—or risk defeat. If the president does not choose compromise, the nominee will go before the committee knowing that he or she must somehow satisfy a majority seeking commitments on specific matters and willing to use every refusal to answer questions as an exhibit in its case in opposition. And critically—unlike in the past, when the segregationists could demand satisfaction but could only stall and whine if they did not get it—the demands for these commitments will come from a majority capable of preventing the nominee from garnering confirmation. A conservative nominee who stood today before a Democratic Senate and delivered a declaration concerning *Roe* akin to the one Potter Stewart made of *Brown*—"I would not like you to vote for me [believing] I am for preserving that decision, because I am not. I have no pre-judgment for that decision"—simply would not command a majority vote. A nominee who professed belief, as Thurgood Marshall did, in a living Constitution before a Republican Senate would similarly get voted down. This formula is a recipe for the extraction of commitments from nominees.

As long as the parties remain so divided on judges and the Senate so firmly behind its prerogative of substantive interrogation, this Catch-22 can only resolve in one of two ways. Either nominees will have to begin offering precisely the kind of assurances they have since 1955 refused to give or the Senate will begin voting many more nominees down even in the absence of plausible allegations against them. The pressure on nominees is already substantial. Roberts was particularly troubled by some of his courtesy calls on individual senators, of which he paid around eighty. "Many of them just wanted to be one-on-one. Fine, I understand that," he told me. "But now what is it you want—now that you've got me alone? And in many cases it was just for more private and therefore more sincere expressions of good wishes. . . . And in other cases it's just a little more awkward. You know, I'm still not going to tell you what I'm going to do. Now that we're alone, I'm still not going to tell you how I'm going to vote."

A greater willingness on the part of nominees to telescope their views would be an enormous change. Roberts says that a nominee who gave away anything substantial at a hearing would, at the Supreme Court, "be regarded as different" for it, and he expressed relief that Alito had not done so.[6] His point is by no means a partisan one. Ginsburg, who as a nominee coined the famous demurral "no hints, no forecasts, no previews," publicly endorsed Roberts's reticence at his hearing, declaring it in a speech to be "unquestionably right."[7] It is a sobering prospect that the logic of our current rules demands that we reject nominees for acting in a fashion the judiciary quite uniformly regards as correct—at least judging by the way sitting judges of both parties have behaved before the committee. If Ginsburg is right and the nominee's obligation is so clear, it is an absurd dilemma in which to place nominees, and ultimately one corrosive of judicial independence,

to require them as a matter of course to compromise either themselves or their prospects.

The entire history of the questioning of nominees testifies to
Ginsburg's correctness. For if that history proves anything, it proves
that the very purpose of these interrogations is, and always has
been, either to wring concessions from would-be justices or to tar
them as unworthy. The goal has never been to inquire into judicial
philosophy out of senators' profound abstract concerns for legal
questions—though senators have certainly been known to pose as
experts in constitutional law. Rather, senators have always sought
to pressure nominees either to deliver the goods or to seem un-
cooperative, either to swear allegiance to a particular set of ideas
being actively contested in court or to offer opponents a ready
ground for their opposition. And that is exactly what the hearings
do. They function coercively not because they are failing to fulfill
their intended purposes but precisely because they *are* fulfilling
them. In a profound sense, Roberts is quite wrong to suggest that
hearings featuring a nominee's testimony could be different. They
could, but that would defeat the purpose.

As long as senators have sought to probe the views of nominees,
they have also sought to draw a distinction between explicitly questioning them about their future votes and questioning them about
past cases. As Senator Schumer put it in his opening statement at
the Roberts hearings, "having established that ideology and judicial
philosophy are important, what's the best way to go about questioning on these subjects? The best way, I believe, is through understanding your views about particular past cases, not future cases
that haven't been decided, but past, already-decided cases. . . .
Some have argued that questioning a nominee about his or her
personal views of the Constitution or about decided cases indicates
prejudgment about a future case. It does nothing of the sort."[8]

This is, of course, the same argument that Senator McClellan
made in the Potter Stewart hearings when he demanded that the

nominee address the merits of *Brown.* McClellan emphasized to Stewart that he had not asked "how you would decide a case, even under the same state of facts, nor have I asked you whether you would feel bound by that decision. I simply wanted to . . . get the philosophy and the ideas of the man as an individual."[9] I do not mean here to draw any moral equivalence between contemporary questioning of nominees and the attempt by Southern senators to bully nominees into keeping their hands off an evil way of life, but it is important to appreciate that the intellectual equivalence is almost exact. This approach has acquired a great deal of academic legitimacy in the intervening years, but it is no righter now than it was then—for the simple reason that there exists no appropriate way for a nominee to answer such questions without eroding his or her later maneuvering room.

Take *Roe v. Wade,* the case whose preservation or elimination has formed a big part of the heart and soul of every nomination hearing since Bork's. In Schumer's formulation, it is a past case, one that has already been decided, and there is no good reason a nominee cannot, while declining to say whether he or she would vote to overturn it, state a view on whether the court decided it properly as an original matter. Everyone, after all, has such views. Getting a nominee to state them surely offers a better window on that person's judicial thinking than eliciting platitudes about deciding cases according to the facts and the law. And for a nominee such as Bork or Ginsburg, both of whom had publicly stated their views on the subject long before their nominations, the issue can be manageable. Bork, for example, stood by his earlier criticism of the right to privacy as articulated in *Griswold v. Connecticut* as "a free-floating right that was not derived in a principled fashion from constitutional materials" and of *Roe* specifically as containing "almost no legal reasoning" that "roots the right to an abortion in constitutional materials."[10] Ginsburg, for her part, stood by her earlier criticisms of the reasoning and breadth of *Roe,* as well as her conviction that abortion rights are constitutionally protected. "The decision whether or not to bear a child is central to a woman's life, to her well-being and dignity," she testified. "It is a decision she must make for herself. When Government controls that decision for her, she is being treated as less than a fully adult human responsible for her own choices."[11]

Yet consider the question from the perspective of a nominee who has never stated a public position on *Roe*, be she a private supporter or opponent of the decision. If she says, under oath, that she believes the court decided the case correctly as an original matter, she has effectively promised her vote—that is, she could not then vote to overrule it without seeming to violate a sworn statement to a Senate committee, a statement on which some senators will have explicitly predicated their votes to confirm her. In doing so, she guarantees a considerable structural injustice to any pro-life litigant or state attorney general who might have to argue a future case in defense of an abortion restriction. Are these parties not entitled to adjudication by someone who has not, without benefit of briefing or any elements of the judicial process, publicly sworn to reject their position?

Legal philosopher Ronald Dworkin gives this argument the back of his hand. Alito, he writes derisively, "could have expressed his present opinion on general and controversial issues of constitutional principle and then added that of course his mind is not closed, that he would read and listen with care to any argument offered to show him that he should change his mind. The justices now on the Court have all taken explicit positions on recurring issues; they are not telling anyone to go away."[12]

But a nominee who would tip her hand on the merits of *Roe* would situate herself profoundly differently from judges who have stated a view on a legal question in the course of ruling on prior cases. Leave aside for a moment that judges, by the nature of their jobs, cannot avoid stating their views. In ruling on cases, they presumably have had the benefit of full briefing, oral arguments, and a fully developed factual record. Similarly, an academic who has written on a subject has, one would hope, studied it carefully. When Bork and Ginsburg announced their views, they were therefore announcing their considered views, as Ginsburg, in fact, made clear in explaining at her hearing why she was willing to discuss abortion but not capital punishment: "I have written about [abortion], I have spoken about it as a teacher since the middle seventies. You know that teaching and appellate judging are more alike than any two ways of working at the law. I tried to be scholarly in my approach to the question then. I have written law review articles."[13] A nominee who, by contrast, shoots from the hip in order to satisfy the committee jettisons the judicial process.

Our hypothetical nominee, of course, as Dworkin suggests, could hedge the point: She could stress that her mind remains open, that her view remains tentative, and that she has never studied the issue with particular care—but nonetheless indicate her preliminary instinct. This course may lessen the damage, but it does not eliminate it. The nominee would then merely have sworn an instinctive prejudice against a position, rather than an absolute prejudice against it. More broadly, it makes no sense to regard such prevarication as the proper response to a question we deem appropriate. If the question is legitimate, the nominee ought to be able to answer it directly.

Breyer took a slightly different tack. He testified that he regarded *Roe*, after the Court's reaffirmation of its core principle in *Planned Parenthood v. Casey*, as "settled law."[14] This may have been defensible when Breyer did it, in the immediate aftermath of *Casey*, which had given *Roe* the sudden blessing of three key Republican appointees to the high court. Breyer chose his words carefully; they do not reveal whether he meant "settled law" descriptively or normatively—that is, whether he meant to indicate that he regarded the controversy as essentially over as an empirical matter or whether he meant that the Court ought not revisit the question. A nominee today would have a harder time giving such an answer. As a descriptive matter, the statement is less true today than it was in 1994. Conservative justices have, after all, emphasized since then that *Casey* did not, in their minds, put the question to rest.[15] So a nominee who said today what Breyer said would unambiguously tip her hand on specific votes—which Breyer almost did in any event. The nominee who believes in *Roe*, in short, has no way to answer the question without effectively doing what no nominee in history has ever done: announcing how she will vote.

The nominee who believes *Roe* wrongly decided arguably has a bit more space to speak. She could, after all, declare her view that the Court got the case wrong as an original matter but refuse to address the question of whether now, more than thirty years after it came down, it deserves deference under the doctrine of *stare decisis*. Here, at least on the surface, she has preserved her options as to how to vote in any future case. But only sort of. For one thing, she has publicly taken a giant intellectual step in the direction of overturning *Roe*. A pro-choice litigant before her would have no meaningful opportunity to make the first argument any lawyer would, under normal circumstances, in defense of a long-standing precedent of the Court: that the justices should not revisit it because of its correctness. Moreover, such a stance would unambiguously tip the nominee's hand on matters far beyond the case at hand. *Roe*, after all, does not exist in a vacuum. It represents part of a line of cases, beginning with *Griswold*, that articulate a privacy right whose full parameters remain very much in dispute. Litigants have unsuccessfully attempted to extend the *Roe* right into a right to doctor-assisted suicide and have successfully sought to extend it to preclude criminal sodomy statutes.[16] A nominee who declared her hostility toward the underlying case, even if she did not promise to attempt its destruction, probably would forecast hostility toward broadening the right it proclaimed.[17]

The only nominee who could actually answer this question honestly is one who genuinely did not know the answer to it. The trouble for this nominee, as Clarence Thomas learned when he professed at his hearings not to recall having discussed *Roe* in law school, never to have debated its merits since, and not to have made "a decision one way or the other" in his own mind about the case, is that many Americans do not regard professed ignorance on the question as an acceptable response from someone headed to the highest court in the land.[18]

Indeed, as Thomas's case also vividly illustrates, the structure of the current mode of questioning encourages nothing so much as disingenuousness and misleading testimony. Thomas, after all, told the committee that he believed in a constitutional right to privacy, that he accepted *stare decisis* as an important principle in constitutional cases, that he had "no quarrel" with the Court's commerce clause jurisprudence, and that he had no ambitions to radically alter the Court's economic rights jurisprudence.[19] His subsequent judicial record has borne out none of these statements. One can choose to believe that Thomas changed his mind with time, to believe that he simply lied, or to believe something in between. It is hard to escape the notion, however, that a senator who relied on his testimony has reason now to feel a certain buyer's remorse.

Roberts, Alito, and Justice David Souter all tried variants of the same script on abortion—embracing the existence of a right to privacy, refusing to express a specific view of *Roe*, and stating general regard for *stare decisis*. That the script is essentially meaningless is clear from the contrast between the subsequent careers of Souter and Thomas. For Souter, provoking a great sense of betrayal on the part of conservatives, it turned out to mean ultimate comfort with *Roe*, even willingness to extend the right to privacy to sodomy laws. Roberts and Alito, having said more or less the same thing, will ultimately be taken to account by one side or the other. Both reserved their options carefully. Yet both also conveyed at once a conservative judicial policy alongside a reverence for precedent and a great appreciation of the weight that time and repeated judicial reaffirmation have placed behind constitutionalized abortion rights. However they eventually vote, a lot of people will feel misled.

Justice Antonin Scalia attempted still a different strategy: a blanket refusal to address any case from any time in history. Scalia not only refused to say what he would do with *Roe*, he refused to engage on the question of privacy at all. He jovially took the same position with respect to *Marbury v. Madison*. (He noted in doing so, however, that "To the extent that you think a nominee would be so foolish, or so extreme, as to kick over one of the pillars of the Constitution, I suppose you should not confirm him" and went on to say that "If you could conclude from anything I have written, or anything I have said, that I would ignore *Marbury v. Madison*, I would too be in trouble.")[20] It was certainly principled. But it is also untenable—at least in the current context. Scalia only got away with it because Democrats were not opposing his nomination but rather concentrating their efforts on attempting to defeat Rehnquist's contemporaneous elevation to chief justice. A nominee who tried this strategy today would inspire the wrath of both sides of the aisle, and none since the flamboyant Scalia has dared. In short, a nominee faced with the *Roe* question—and by extension with many others involving the viability of a contested precedent—cannot directly answer the question and cannot refuse to answer it. Her only real option is to offer pablum that satisfies nobody in the short run and risks angering everybody in the long run.

The impossible position of the nominee has grown even worse with the growth of procedural obstructions, which took off in earnest for lower-court judges at the end of the first Bush administration and then exploded during the Clinton years. Now, in a meaningful sense, the majority of the Senate does not even have to act to hold a nomination hostage based on a nominee's views—or his anticipated views. Individual home-state senators can do it, using the "blue slip" procedure, as long as their party controls the Senate and the committee.[21] The Judiciary Committee chairman has almost unlimited ability to stall for any reason—a power of which both Orrin Hatch and Patrick Leahy made prodigious use against presidents of the opposite party. And the Democratic use of the filibuster presages an even more dramatic escalation: the ability of the *minority* party to stop nominees who do not answer questions. The compromise in 2005 among a bipartisan group of fourteen senators to preserve the filibuster by ensuring that Democrats do not use it often leaves open the question of whether this particular tactic will become, as others have, a routine part of the confirmation process. If it does, the old *Times* editorial will actually have understated the threat. It will no longer be enough for a nominee to "to satisfy the majority of the Senate Judiciary Committee that he was in line" with its view. He may have to satisfy some bloc of the minority as well.

So far, as I have noted, the problem has not dramatically encumbered Supreme Court confirmations—though it has made for lots of unpleasant atmospherics. But at the lower-court level the problem has already become acute, and these nominations offer a vision of where Supreme Court nominations may be headed. Numerous men and women of obvious merit in both parties do not sit on the bench today because senators suspected they harbored views different from their own—often on the flimsiest of evidence—or simply because they had been nominated by the other side. These include the dean of the Harvard Law School, Elena Kagan; high-quality Washington lawyers such as Allen Snyder and Miguel Estrada; former Justice Department officials; and any number of district court judges, state judges, and attorneys in private practice around the country. Not all of these nominees, to be sure, failed to win confirmation specifically because their testimony proved inadequately reassuring to committee members—though that was clearly part of what happened to Estrada. Indeed, many nominees saw the process stall before they received a hearing at all. The real action, particularly during the Clinton years, often involved non-public machinations over when nominations moved, rather than any public questioning. The modalities of the struggle have changed depending upon the temporal balance of power in the Senate. Republicans during the Clinton presidency, having control of the committee and Senate floor for six of eight years, generally buried nominees using procedural obstructions, rather than making public cases against them. Democrats during the Bush years have been more apt to fight publicly; being the minority most of the time, their levers have been limited, leaving the fili-buster, which requires making a public case, as their principal tool.

The constant, however, has been the shift to the nominee of the burden of proving his or her worthiness to a Senate unready to act in the absence of satisfaction, a shift that can create an irresolvable conflict for the conscientious nominee: He or she can-not provide what the Senate wants without either ceding to its members some little bit of his or her ability to decide controversial cases or misleadingly appearing to do so.

I do not mean to overstate the problem. Nominees still get confirmed, and they still generally get confirmed without compro-mising themselves. But they do not do so predictably—and we can confidently foresee that confirmation will grow substantially less predictable during the next period of divided government or during the next period in which the minority party feels confident the filibuster will, if used, not get eliminated as a weapon in its arsenal. We should worry, therefore, that the logic of the Alito vote will not prove fleeting in Supreme Court nominations but a vision of a future reflecting the process as we have constructed it. We should worry, in other words, that the trend is dangerous and that the steep slope we are slipping down has few potential footholds remaining.

The spectacle of the modern confirmation hearing greatly compounds this worry. Such grand political theater, after all, sends a message to the public about congressional expectations of the judiciary and, indeed, about law itself. The message in recent years has been impossible to mistake: It has reflected contempt for the notion that judges of opposing parties may nonetheless endeavor to decide cases neutrally, and it has treated the task of judging merely as an exercise of raw political power. To the extent that the public comes to believe this caricature, the prophecy will tend to fulfill itself. For as law students imbibe such a cynical attitude toward the discipline they are supposedly learning, it infiltrates the profession itself—a fact that makes the participation of law professors in these hearings especially disturbing. We cannot have independent courts without believing in them, after all. And the spectacle of the modern nomination process, even while pressuring the would-be judge on substantive questions, teaches the public a deep disregard for his task.

There exists another, broader threat to judicial independence that warrants consideration in light of the Senate's aggressiveness on confirmations. It is, I concede at the outset, inherently more speculative and uncertain than the immediate problem I have just described, yet it is also potentially far more sweeping and troubling than the Catch-22 for nominees and the accompanying abridgment of the presidential power to name judges. We need to ask whether the breakdown of one key norm that has protected the independence of American courts presages or may even precipitate the breakdown of other norms that serve the same function.

The Constitution's actual guarantees of judicial independence, while substantial, do not remotely approximate the practical guarantees that have built up over the centuries. The Constitution itself promises judges life tenure conditioned on their "good Behavior," and it promises pay "which shall not be diminished during their Continuance in Office."[22] On its own, it promises no more. Yet supporting these explicit guarantees is a set of norms without which we would scarcely recognize the judicial branch. One of these is that Congress, in addition to not cutting the pay of judges, does not leverage its budgetary powers over the judiciary as a whole to push for particular substantive outcomes. Another is that, since the early years of the Republic, it has not used impeachment as a means of either pressuring or punishing judges for particular results. A third is that Congress does not engage in issue-based "court stripping"—that is, it does not use its powers under Article III to create "exceptions" and "regulations" to the Supreme Court's appellate jurisdiction to keep it from ruling on issues concerning which the legislators do not agree with the justices' views. The fourth, for most of American history, has been a certain modesty in the confirmation process—the idea that in minding the gateways to the courts, Congress does not condition a nominee's confirmation on substantive concessions.

It is important to stress again that this modesty in the confirmation process was always a matter of norm, never of law. Though the norm certainly has roots in values the Constitution describes, the Constitution's actual description of the Senate's role does not compel it. The words "Advice and Consent" are as consistent with robust, ideologically driven inquest and veto as with a deferential and brief examination of qualifications and temperament. The occasional argument, generally advanced by conservatives during the current Bush administration, that the modern system—particularly the filibuster—suffers from some constitutional infirmity is surely wrong.[23] Rather, it seems to fit comfortably within a vaguely worded textual grant of power, as did the system that preceded it, as well as the freewheeling power struggles that took place over nominations during the nineteenth century.[24] Only in the most general sense does the Constitution itself regulate the confirmation

process; regulating it in actual operation is the Senate's own sense
of propriety and sense of its place in relation to the courts.

That sense is also what really inhibits congressional adventur-
ism with respect to budgetary pressures, court-stripping measures,
and impeachments. At least on its face, after all, the Constitution
would not prevent conservative appropriators from cutting the Supreme Court's budget in retaliation for some case reaffirming *Roe*
or stop liberal appropriators from prospectively denying the Court
the funds necessary to hear a case that might overturn *Roe*. Nor
does the Constitution itself prohibit Congress from treating aggressive decisions with which members passionately disagree as
"high crimes and misdemeanors" for purposes of the impeachment
power. Indeed, this understanding of the Constitution caught on
only at the time of the impeachment of Justice Samuel Chase,
whom the Senate acquitted in 1805. As Chief Justice Rehnquist
put it in a charming history of the Chase and Andrew Johnson
impeachments, the Chase acquittal "had a profound effect on the
American judiciary," assuring "the independence of federal judges
from congressional oversight of the decisions they made in the
cases that came before them" and that "impeachment would not
be used in the future as a method to remove members of the
Supreme Court for their judicial opinions."[25] But there is no reason, other than ongoing respect for these values, why Congress
could not now act differently. Court-stripping measures present a
somewhat trickier case, for the validity of laws restricting the courts'
jurisdiction over constitutional cases itself represents one of the
great open questions of constitutional law. Yet this reality only per-
sists because the norm against congressional meddling with the
courts' jurisdiction has proved so strong. Despite whining from the
Right when the Court veers to the left and whining from the Left
when the Court lurches right, Congress—with notable exceptions—has generally not tested its power to frustrate judicial review.

History, to be sure, records dissenters from each of these areas of congressional restraint. Movements to impeach Earl Warren and William O. Douglas famously cropped up, for example, and Strom Thurmond suggested impeaching justices at Marshall's hearings.[26] Court-stripping measures have also been proposed in recent decades, on school busing, abortion, the Pledge of Allegiance, and lots of other matters. As the Roberts hearings brought out, in fact, the Reagan administration split internally over whether to endorse court-stripping, with Roberts, then a political appointee in the attorney general's office, urging the legitimacy of such measures and then-Assistant Attorney General Theodore B. Olson arguing against them.[27] Yet as with senatorial restraint on confirmations over many years, these norms persisted in the face of whatever calls were made for their erosion.

We must now question whether these norms will prove to have stronger legs than did the norm of restraint in the confirmation process—and whether we care if they do not. The latter part of this question seems easy to answer: A world in which the legislature removed judges it did not like, leveraged the judiciary's budget into substantive results, and allowed the courts to consider only those questions it wished heard would not make for a hospitable climate for the rule of law and independent justice. The first element of the question, however, is harder. The collapse of one of a table's legs, after all, need not precipitate the collapse of the others, and some tables can stand stably on three legs. It would be alarmist to declare confidently that the entire table is on the verge of collapse.

Yet the deterioration of the nomination process at least raises the question of whether we are heading in this direction. If one believes, as I have argued, that the confirmation process has changed as an institutional reaction on the part of the legislature to the growth of the power of the judiciary, it stands to reason that the legislature would, in the long run, also make use of other levers at its disposal to strengthen its hand.

There is at least some evidence this is already happening—far from conclusive evidence, but troubling nonetheless. For starters, Congress has actually passed a string of court-stripping measures over the past several years, albeit not of the most provocative sort. In 1996, it passed two big ones, a habeas corpus reform law that precluded many habeas petitions and an immigration reform law that blocked judicial review of many administrative judgments against illegal immigrants facing deportation.[28] In 2005 it passed a bill to overturn the high court's assertion of jurisdiction over habeas corpus actions from those held as enemy combatants at the Guantanamo Bay naval base in Cuba.[29] Congressional meddling with the Court's habeas jurisdiction represents, to be sure, a somewhat less dramatic intrusion than, say, an effort to create an exception to its general appellate jurisdiction to hear a specified set of constitutional questions. In a formal sense, after all, Congress is merely tinkering with jurisdiction it had granted in passing the federal habeas statute in the first place, a statute the Court had interpreted far more broadly in the Guantanamo case than before.[30] This point conceded, Congress is clearly taking a more aggressive posture than in the past—particularly in the Guantanamo case. Faced with a Court that regarded itself as confronted with substantial constitutional and treaty questions it had the power to hear, the legislature essentially declared, "Oh, no, you don't."

This declaration did not occur in a vacuum. The House of Representatives has passed far more aggressive court-stripping bills in recent years—bills that would deny the Supreme Court the ability to hear cases on the Pledge of Allegiance and gay marriage.[31] And both houses of Congress have contemplated bills to radically curtail federal habeas corpus in capital cases as well.[32]

Moreover, the Guantanamo bill followed less than a year after the Terri Schiavo incident, in which Congress affirmatively passed a law to give the federal courts jurisdiction to hear a specific case—and deliver a specific result—and then exploded in rage when the courts nonetheless refused. Schiavo was a Florida woman in a persistent vegetative state; the Florida courts had permitted her husband to disconnect her from life support over the objections of her parents. After the federal courts refused to get involved in what was quite obviously a state matter, Congress passed a special measure to force them to consider the case.[33] The courts, including some very conservative judges, nonetheless declined to jump in, there being no plausible constitutional infringement to correct.[34] Members of Congress, including then-House Majority Leader Tom DeLay, responded with explicit threats. "This loss happened because our legal system did not protect the people who need protection most, and that will change," DeLay said. "The time will come for the men responsible for this to answer for their behavior, but not today."[35] Even in apologizing later for this remark, DeLay did not back off its substance—the ability of Congress to rein in the courts. He did not forswear impeachment as a potential remedy for judicial decisions he disliked. Indeed, he referred the whole matter to the House Judiciary Committee for examination. Nor did he forswear jurisdiction-stripping measures. "We set the jurisdiction of the courts," he said. "We set up the courts. We can unset the courts."[36] DeLay even gave the keynote speech, by video, to a conference entitled "Confronting the Judicial War on Faith," in which he decried "a judiciary run amok" and promised, "Our next step, whatever it is, must be more than rhetoric."[37]

DeLay is far from the only political figure to have suggested the use of a fuller panoply of congressional powers to get what the majority wants from judges. In House appropriations subcommittee hearings on the judiciary's budget in 2005, for example, Kansas Republican Todd Tiahrt lectured two justices and a federal appeals court judge on his irritation with the courts' independence and all but stated a link to the budgetary matters the subcommittee had before it. "You know, we don't ask much from the courts. We just pay the bills," he said. Then, in an apparent reference to Schiavo, he complained that "The one time that we did ask something from the courts, a simple judicial review of the facts of a case, we were ignored."[38]

The House Judiciary Committee, under the leadership of Chairman James Sensenbrenner, is also taking a more aggressive posture toward the investigation of federal judges. Sometimes it has focused on purported ethical questions. Committee staff members expended significant energy, for example, in investigating the sentencing practices and the veracity of testimony by James M. Rosenbaum, a district judge in Minnesota.[39] It also looked into alleged manipulations of the Sixth Circuit's handling of an affirmative action case.[40] It investigated a leak to the press by Judge Richard Cudahy of the U.S. Court of Appeals for the Seventh Circuit in connection with an independent counsel investigation — and Sensenbrenner filed an ethics complaint concerning it.[41] But Sensenbrenner has not always even maintained the line between investigating supposed ethical infractions and substantive disagreements with the judges over whom he conducts oversight. Thus, for example, he wrote a letter to the chief judge of the Seventh Circuit complaining about Judge Frank Easterbrook's handling of a routine criminal sentencing appeal, then still pending, and demanded that the chief judge take "all necessary and appropriate measures . . . to ensure . . . a lawful sentence in this case."[42] Sensenbrenner has insisted upon the legitimacy of court-stripping measures as well.[43]

All of this may prove to be merely fringe political rhetoric. Right now, it is confined almost entirely to the Right and engenders not a little embarrassment among many mainstream conservatives, including the Bush administration. Such talk has, as I have noted, arisen before and not caught on. Perhaps the same will happen again.

But the collapse of the confirmation norm at least gives us reason to worry. For one thing, the majority leader of the House and the chairman of the House Judiciary Committee almost by definition do not constitute the fringe. We dismiss their rhetoric, even if they currently lack the power to effectuate it, at our peril. A wing of the conservative movement is talking quite seriously about dramatically escalating the legislature's war with the federal courts. I see no reason why those who value the traditional allocations of power between the branches should not take them at their word about what they mean to do. Moreover, as the history of the confirmation process demonstrates, what lies on the fringe today can get adopted by the political culture awfully quickly. The idea of questioning judges, after all, was similarly fringy, until liberals and moderates found themselves with the power and incentive to engage in it themselves and with strong precedents they could cite as justification—at which point they turned on a dime. What basis for confidence do we really have that these other norms will prove any more resilient than the one against aggressive questioning of nominees?

I venture the guess that the correct answer to this question is that we have no basis for confidence—other than the fact that a court-stripping, budget-abusing, impeachment-wielding Congress appears to many reasonable people nowadays the height of legislative impropriety, just as a Senate that grilled a Supreme Court nominee on substantive questions was unthinkable only a few decades ago. Put another way, the same growth of judicial power and influence in policy matters that caused an institutional rethinking of the Senate's approach to confirmations could drive a much broader and more aggressive congressional response. While I am not, at this point, prepared to predict that events will inexorably move in that direction, we ought to worry about the possibility even while we object in the immediate term to the bind in which the current process puts nominees.

CHAPTER 5

■

Conclusion: A Confirmation Process for Angry Times

Can we do anything to restore the confirmation process to health and forestall erosion of these other normative protections for judicial independence? Almost certainly not—if by this question we imply some nostalgic longing for a more collegial time. We cannot wave away the concerns that judicial power raises, nor should we try. The judiciary, like any governmental power center, needs checks on its power; those checks can only grow in rigor as the judiciary's power increases. Indeed, throughout the twentieth century, there have been few moments when judges were not pursuing a project their opponents derided as activism—whether that project was Lochnerism, the rights revolution of the Warren and Burger Courts, or what I would call the modern Court's centrist aggressiveness. My purpose here is not a sociological assessment of why Americans want such a strong judiciary. But it seems highly implausible that, more than a century after *Lochner*, a reasonable analysis of this type would dismiss the entirety—or even the majority—of the judicial energy of the past hundred years as a usurpation of power in abject defiance of popular will. That is not the way democracy works. At some level, we have had such broad judicial power because people want it. And as long as the American love affair with judicial power continues, the legislature will respond in some way; that is what the separation of powers is all about.

For precisely this reason, the vast majority of proposed solutions to the "confirmation mess," as Stephen Carter calls it, seem doomed to failure. Consider, first, what we might term the cultural solutions—which, to one degree or another, seek a kind of unilateral judicial disarmament. The idea has two broad iterations, one flowing from the conservative narrative, the other more politically neutral. The conservative version posits that only a return to some version of originalism can restore comity to the process. The more neutral version, typified by Carter, asks generally for a less grandiose vision of the Court—thereby letting some of the air out of the confirmation balloon.

Judicial modesty is a point of a high principle, one for which I have great sympathy, but as I have suggested earlier, history has not proved it much of a prescription. This is, after all, what the judicial Right has argued for since *Brown*. Yet nearly two decades of the Rehnquist Court have not seemed very modest to liberals infuriated over federalism and, particularly, *Bush v. Gore*. Nor, for that matter, has it seemed particularly modest to many conservatives, who remain almost as irate today about judicial behavior as they were at the height of the Warren Court. Indeed, judicial modesty is a virtue whose parameters our society agrees upon so little that seeing a solution in it is really akin to observing that we could all agree if only we could all agree. So while one can hope that Roberts and Alito will both act strictly according to the principles of modesty they professed in their confirmation proceedings, we should not imagine that such fidelity will cure much. Consider only one example: Roberts cast his first dissenting vote on the Court in a case testing whether the attorney general had the power to use federal drug laws to frustrate Oregon's law on doctor-assisted suicide. The majority held that he did not have this power; Roberts would have held that he did.[1] Roberts probably saw this vote as fully in keeping with a modest conception of the judicial function. The dissenters were arguing for deference to an executive branch reading of federal law. Liberals, however, took it as a sign of aggressive conservatism; he was, after all, voting to allow federal power to interfere with a state-level policy initiative to which social conservatives objected.[2] If this dispute seems like a plausible vision of the future, we should be modest about modesty's capacity to solve this problem.

Another category of possible reforms involves some measure of unilateral disarmament on the part of the Senate, that is, changes to the Senate rules and procedures that would facilitate quicker consideration of nominations. President Bush proposed such reforms in 2002.[3] Democrats made similar noises during Clinton's presidency. Most famously, Republicans sought to do away with the filibuster in 2005, a move aborted by the deal announced by the bipartisan group of fourteen senators. Reform of Senate rules to eliminate abuses of Senate procedures and to set reasonable timetables for Senate action could go a long way toward solving the problem. The trouble is that there exists no obvious mechanism for getting the Senate to so emasculate itself. One can imagine a temporary majority eliminating the filibuster, though even this has proved very difficult. But the filibuster, despite its high profile, has never been the core of the problem; while the possibility of its profligate use certainly poses grave concerns, senators have so far stopped only a few nominees using it. The problem has not generally been manipulations by the minority party but the *majority's* ability to stall and stop nominees of a president of the opposite party. Why would either party give up this power?

Two potential answers come to mind. The first is that one party, in a period of unified government, might decide to strengthen the president's hand by altering the rules. But neither party has carried enough legislative strength to accomplish this feat in recent years, and it hardly seems likely in the near future. Nor is it clear that a party that had such a large majority would bother. It would have the strength to move judges at whatever speed it wanted. Why give away the power to block the president's nominees in times of lesser parliamentary strength? The second possibility is that senators might, in a moment of high-minded patriotism, reform the rules in such a fashion that the changes would go into effect at some time in the future—some time when nobody knows which side would control the White House or the Senate. The idea would be that legislating from behind a veil of ignorance as to which side would win or lose by reform would enable both sides to imagine the public interest, rather than their own immediate political interests. Such a deal is an attractive possibility but probably a remote one, for it asks senators of both parties to give away the power of their institution—and therefore defies the basic structural truth of "Federalist No. 51" that institutions tend to concentrate power to themselves, not push it away. Exceptions exist—congressional passage of the line-item veto, for example. But they are exceptions. In the main, one can expect the Senate to behave over time in precisely the opposite of the fashion envisioned by this scenario—that is, to arrange its rules so as to maximize the opportunity for its majority to influence the choice of judges and justices.

Liberals and conservatives have also helpfully suggested, when they are not in control of the White House, a kind of unilateral presidential disarmament. Conservatives urged Clinton to stop appointing liberal judges, for example, and liberals have demanded of successive conservative presidents that they preserve the "balance" of the courts. Such ideas go nowhere, for much the same reason that the Senate does not rein in its own role. People do not run for president—the office in fact tasked with appointing judges—in order to name those of an opposing philosophical persuasion. Presidents take such steps only when forced or when some significant political benefit might accrue to them as a consequence.

This brings us to the next broad category of possible solution—a kind of mutually beneficial political accord that offers both the presidency and the Senate sufficient advantage to sign on. Generally, the idea is that the president would agree to augment prenomination consultation with the Senate in exchange for quicker, smoother confirmation for his nominees, perhaps formalized in more reasonable Senate rules. I have hoped for such an accord for years, across two administrations of opposite party, and I remain somewhat puzzled as to why it has never materialized. Glimpses of how it would work have arisen at times—for example, in the relationship between Clinton and Hatch in the early phase of Republican control over the Senate. Clinton listened to Hatch's warnings concerning which lower-court nominees would provoke confrontations with his caucus. For his part, Hatch sometimes energetically went to bat for Clinton nominees—most prominently for Merrick Garland.[4] Bush, on taking office, took some steps to try to smooth ruffled Democratic feathers—reappointing Roger Gregory, whom Clinton had placed on the Fourth Circuit using a recess appointment after Senator Jesse Helms had serially blocked Clinton's appointments to that court, and elevating liberal District Judge Barrington Parker Jr. to the Second Circuit.

In both Clinton's case and Bush's, however, the efforts at collaboration broke down. Hatch was never able to deliver broader cooperation from the Republican caucus, which even tried to rein in his powers as chairman to stop his accommodations. In Clinton's second term, Hatch gave up the effort. And his relationship with the White House faltered further over a patronage dispute involving a Utah judgeship. Bush's efforts to set a new tone were altogether half-hearted. The Parker and Gregory appointments were a one-shot deal from a White House generally keen to maximize presidential prerogatives in the nominations process and elsewhere. Nor did Democrats reciprocate with speedy treatment of Bush's initial crop of nominees. Ultimately, both presidents preferred the status of wounded combatant to bipartisan leader on this score. Clinton chose not to invest much political energy in his judges. And Bush chose to use the treatment of his judges as a campaign issue—quite successfully—rather than seek accord.

One could imagine a future president acting differently—say, beginning his term by renominating the wronged appointees of both of his predecessors and then asking the Senate to treat his nominees differently in the future. But in the current political environment, this course has the feel of a noble fantasy, not a realistic plan of action. After all the nasty things Democrats said about Estrada, for example, a Democratic president is just not going to renominate him, even if he would be willing to accept the appointment. Political scientist Nancy Scherer's work identifies part of the reason: If judgeships are ideology-advancing devices, it is far harder to compromise on them with people of the opposing ideology than if they represent patronage devices, in which case a nearly 900-member judiciary offers enough patronage opportunities to go around. We can retain the hope that some president of either party will see statesmanship as enlightened self-interest and that such a president could embarrass the opposing party into reciprocity. But we should concede that this is both unlikely to happen and far from certain, if it ever does happen, to succeed.

Still others have suggested judicial elections as the optimal reform. The idea, as political scientist Richard Davis put it in his recent book, *Electing Justice*, is to "formalize a public role while limiting the ability of the news media or groups to claim the mantle of public representative and spokesperson." Rather than ignoring "the democratic changes in the selection process or condemn them, the nation should adjust to them by designing a judicial selection process that matches the democratization present in American politics while securing a judicial branch capable of defending its independence."[5] If that sounds suspiciously like institutionalizing all of the vices of the contemporary process, that is actually not an accident; if we are going to have populism, why not have it for real? As Stephen Carter puts it, judicial elections— either direct, contested elections or referenda on the president's choice—would be "less different from what we do now than they may seem. . . . Were we to elect the Justices directly, rather than by proxy, the principal change would be that this game of democratic checkery, of having the chance to enshrine the values of a passing political majority as fundamental constitutional law, would be opened up to the entire voting public . . . rather than limited to the liberal and conservative Beltway activists who speak with perfect sincerity in the people's name."[6]

Even a brief look at state judicial elections ought to reveal the repugnance of this idea, which would amount to a thorough capitulation to the politicization of courts. Put simply, if one does not want politicians as judges, one should not make judges run for their offices. That current political campaigns around nominations sometimes bear an unnerving similarity to an electoral campaign hardly justifies turning them into the real thing.

Finally, some commentators have advanced the idea of a supermajority requirement for confirmation—thereby ensuring that presidents will consult out-party sentiment and nominate relative centrists to the Court.[7] Like judicial elections, this idea is both terrible on its merits and, in any event, nearly impossible to implement. It would require a constitutional amendment and, thereby, at any given time require a considerable number of votes from the party whose power it would diminish. And if it somehow ever did get enacted, it would narrow the range of acceptable judges to the space between Breyer and O'Connor—as each party would be able to compel opposing presidents to accommodate them maximally. For those of us who value the careers of both Justice Scalia and Justice Brennan, this idea carries little appeal.

There exists, in brief, no comprehensive solution to the nominations morass on which to place one's hopes. The forces that have brought American judicial politics to its current state have too great a momentum and internal logic to give way before either earnest pleading or technocratic schemes to depoliticize a system in which both sides maintain substantial political stakes.

Steps do exist, however, that we might envisage to better manage the conflict, steps that do not deny but build on the structural power incentives the process creates for the different branches of government. Specifically, these steps should take advantage of the institutional alignment of the interests of the executive and judicial branches in reining in the confirmation process.

I do not mean here anything as temporary as an alignment of interests between the judiciary and President Bush in particular, but rather between the institution of the judiciary and the institutional presidency more generally. The coincidence of interests here, evident in Chief Justice Rehnquist's advocacy of fair treatment for President Clinton's nominees, transcends partisan politics.[8] The judiciary has a strong interest in nominees not being held hostage to legislative manipulations for long periods or forced to state their positions on issues in a manner that would erode later confidence in their objectivity. The presidency, meanwhile, has an abiding interest in a process in which presidents can get their nominees confirmed in an expeditious and predictable manner. An alliance of convenience between the two already exists to some degree. Recognizing the confluence of interests here and strengthening it into a kind of strategic partnership could help at once to protect judicial nominees against the cruel choice of substantive testimony, non-responsiveness, and prevarication and to prevent further erosions of the norms that otherwise protect the judiciary from legislative encroachments.

Such an alliance would work best if the president and chief justice came from opposing parties; otherwise, it risks displaying a partisan sheen. As a practical matter—since Roberts is young and Republican—this means waiting for a Democratic president. But such a partnership could take critical steps toward improving the process. The most important would be either eliminating—or at least limiting—live testimony of nominees at their hearings.

A few months before Justice O'Connor's retirement was announced and Chief Justice Rehnquist's death, I wrote a brief essay on the history of confirmation proceedings for chief justices, which began with the following, half-joking advice to the Senate Judiciary Committee as it geared up for hearings on Rehnquist's replacement: "Oh, just skip them."[9] Having since reviewed the history of confirmation proceedings far more systematically, I now advance the idea with utter seriousness. Live testimony by nominees represents a historical aberration, born in an original sin from which it has never recovered. It also contributes remarkably little to mature Senate consideration of nominees.

Senator Joseph Biden of Delaware acknowledged this latter point candidly at Alito's hearings, saying to one panel of witnesses, "I must tell you I have diminishing regard for the efficacy of hearings on judicial nominees in terms of getting at the truth."[10] Biden's point is surely correct; we do not learn much about nominees from their testimony. But he draws the wrong conclusion. He means to suggest, with Dworkin, that nominees ought to say more, whereas the defect in fact lies in the hearings themselves, not in any nominee.

Indeed, one struggles to identify a single instance when a Supreme Court nominee's testimony has proved genuinely revealing about his or her future career on the Court. Where no controversy hangs over a nomination, nominee testimony is a most pedestrian affair: Senators do not seek information aggressively and do not object loudly when nominees give up little. We learn nothing, and we do not complain. By contrast, when controversy does surround a nomination, the hearings turn contentious, aggressive, and un-pleasant—and remain uninformative. One can, to be sure, discover information in hearings past that seems relevant in light of subsequent events. Looking at their testimony in retrospect, David Souter does seem to embrace privacy rights more comprehensively than Clarence Thomas.[11] One can discern, perhaps, Scalia's inflexibility and dogmatism in his hard-line refusal to discuss cases with senators. Perhaps Rehnquist's playful repartee, by contrast, suggested the more ecumenical, flexible conservatism he brought to the role of chief justice. But forecasting the past requires no tea leaves.

Indeed, the hearings brought out none of these points adequately for people to appreciate them prior to the Senate's votes to confirm. Souter's testimony may be a bit of an exception; it reassured some observers. New York Times columnist Anthony Lewis even perceptively noted that while "Judge Souter was nominated by a Republican President, presented as a conservative and accepted as such by the conservative movement . . . the approach he spelled out to constitutional judging differs sharply from that of the radical legal right."[12] As Janet Malcolm wrote in the New Yorker after the Alito hearings, "in light of Souter's testimony . . . his opinions on the high court should not have been surprising." Yet the hints notwithstanding, Souter's liberalism was surprising. As Malcolm concedes, her prediction is entirely retroactive: "Souter's record on civil rights, voting rights, gay rights, and victim rights and his bias toward law enforcement was similarly mocked and denounced by the feminists. Had these angry witnesses been able to see into the future, would they have testified as they did? Of course not. And had I not known how things turned out with Souter would I have watched the tape of his confirmation hearing with the same charmed delight? Of course not. We read what we can into reality's impassive face."[13]

Similarly, Scalia, at the time of his nomination, was understood by liberals to be dramatically preferable to Rehnquist; after the testimony of both men, in fact, many observers assumed he would prove more moderate. The *Washington Post*, for example, termed Rehnquist's civil rights record not one "of conservative philosophy, but judicial implacability" while noting that Scalia "does not have a history of inflexibility that would lead us to the same conclusions that we have reached on Justice Rehnquist."[14] Clearly, soliciting both men's testimony proved of marginal value in assessing them. Nor, of course, did John Marshall Harlan turn out to advocate world government. And for all the confident predictions about Alito and Roberts, we did not learn much of consequence about what sort of jurists they will be, either—other than that they will be conservatives of some sort, which we already knew. If the history of confirmation hearings teaches one thing, it teaches great caution in drawing any conclusions based on them.

My point here is not that assessing a nominee rigorously is impossible or that nominees always—or even often—turn out surprising. To the contrary, the Senate generally votes on nominees with a rough sense of who they are: Burger, Rehnquist, Scalia, and Thomas were all conservatives, as Bork surely would have been. Breyer and Ginsburg have turned out more or less as expected as well. Everyone knew Marshall would be a liberal—and he was. O'Connor and Kennedy were understood to be moderate conservatives, as they proved to be. The point, rather, is that the nominees' testimony added virtually nothing to our understanding of these people. Michael Comiskey, perhaps inadvertently, provides an excellent illustration of this point; he devotes an entire chapter of his book to demonstrating that—with Souter as an exception—the "stealth nominee" is largely a myth. Yet in his thorough and convincing discussion of those aspects of the justices' records that forecast their futures on the Court, he makes virtually no mention of their testimony.[15]

Indeed, the Senate debates over Charles Evans Hughes and John Parker in 1930 were conducted at a level dramatically more sophisticated and informed than anything that followed Harlan's hearing in 1955, and all without the benefit of nominee testimony. If the Senate erred in its vote on Parker, it was not for lack of information that would have been corrected had Parker been permitted to answer live for his actions; indeed, the senators made essentially the same misjudgment that their successors made about Clement Haynsworth after three days of questioning him. If progressives underestimated Hughes, they did not misjudge the man because of a lack of opportunity to question him but because he turned out to have a more open mind than they expected. Today, such a nominee would tell the committee as much and refuse to answer detailed questions, and members of the opposite party would disbelieve him and be caught just as off guard as were progressives of the time.

Hearings do offer occasional insights into the character of nominees. One cannot read transcripts of Marshall's hearings without a deep sense of admiration for the man—whose forbearance, seriousness, and dignity in the face of Southern racists bore all the hallmarks of greatness. By contrast, William Brennan did not acquit himself admirably, faced with McCarthy's bullying. Yet here, too, the hearings proved a lousy bellwether. For whatever their personal courage, Brennan surely became a much greater justice than Marshall.

Put simply, one strains to find a single example of a truly useful, probative hearing at which the committee garnered information that proved valuable prospectively in assessing the likely qualities of a nominee as a justice. Souter, in a very limited sense, is one candidate, having sufficiently reassured Democrats that they did not oppose him en masse. But he is the only plausible candidate. Did we really learn anything about Bork that we did not already know—other than the hardly disqualifying facts that his beard looked devilish and his manner put people off? To the contrary, after days of tortuous hearings, the Senate rejected Bork based on a record that existed before they ever began. To the extent that he disavowed that record at the hearings, senators questioned whether his recanting constituted a "confirmation conversion."[16] Any rigorous review of nominee testimony, in my view, must end where nominee testimony started—with the wisdom of Frankfurter's opening remarks at his own appearance in 1939: "[A] nominee's record should be thoroughly scrutinized by this committee [but] I hope you will not think it presumptuous on my part to suggest that neither such examination nor the best interests of the Supreme Court will be helped by the personal participation of the nominee himself."[17]

Getting rid of nominee testimony is not a new idea; it has occasionally cropped up before—and generally been treated as an eccentricity. Criticizing an earlier such recommendation, for example, John Anthony Maltese writes that it suggests "a return to a golden age, when Supreme Court nominees were not required to testify, when the facetious whims of public opinion were ignored by senators, when the legal qualifications of nominees were considered without the taint of political motivation, and when senators deliberated behind closed doors rather than posturing in the glare of television lights. The problem is that the apolitical nature of that golden age is largely fictitious."[18] I do not posit a golden, apolitical age of confirmations. I do, however, suggest that nominee testimony makes matters worse and accomplishes almost nothing along the way.

The peculiarity of the nation's commitment to this tradition is that few observers actually express satisfaction with the informative value of nominee testimony. More typically, the defense involves a healthy dose of acquiescence to its inevitability. This is how we do things now. Stephen Carter, for example, having accurately identified the modern hearings as rooted in the segregationist response to *Brown* and having attacked their content and style for nearly 200 pages, cannot quite bring himself to give them up. "I am no great fan of requiring nominees to testify," he writes, "but at this point in our history, this change would cause more problems than it would solve."[19] I very much doubt this proposition.

I do not hold out the ending of nominee testimony as any kind of cure-all. It would not alter the underlying dynamics, after all. The Court would remain as powerful as it is, senators as anxious about that power and as eager to mind the ideological gates. It would not eliminate unfair mischaracterizations of a nominee's record or the prevalence of interest groups. Eliminating nominee testimony would, in fact, accomplish only one thing—but a huge thing that would have a great clarifying effect on the Senate's process. It would remove the central event to which all of this builds, that opportunity for senators to confront the nominee and, over hours and days of national spectacle, make him or her answerable for every decision the Court has ever made or might make in the future.

It would, in other words, remove what Biden tellingly—and quite wrongly—called during the Alito hearings that "one democratic moment . . . before a lifetime of judicial independence when the people of the United States are entitled to know as much as we can about the person that we're about to entrust with safeguarding our future and the future of our kids."[20] For the one democratic moment is not the interrogation of the nominee, a moment that serves few true democratic ends—except to the extent that creating a forum for the strutting moral pomposity of senators can be considered as such. The true democratic moment is, rather, the point at which the people's representatives actually debate the nominee's record and cast their votes for or against confirmation. And ironically, one of the chief consequences of the hearings process is to detract attention, both public and senatorial attention, from that moment. Many readers, I am sure, remember Alito and Roberts not saying how they will vote on abortion, for example. How many, however, can remember what a single senator said during the floor debate over either of them?

The difficult question is not whether nominee testimony ought to go but what mechanism might enable its abolition. With any given nomination, the path of least resistance for the president and the nominee alike is to cooperate with the committee — or, at least, to appear to cooperate with the committee. If a nominee refused to show up, the Senate would simply decline to move forward. Any effort to alter the lay of the land here would have to attempt change more globally, relieving the individual nominee of the burden of deciding whether to make himself available for questioning. We can surely expect the Senate to resist any such efforts. Yet unlike proposals for reform of Senate rules, which rely on some mysterious decision by senators to do the right thing, there exists an institution with the heft to push hard on this front: the presidency of the United States.

Specifically, a president could simply refuse to let his nominees appear before the committee. He could articulate the reason: that nominee testimony serves no compelling purpose and offers too much capacity for pressure on the nominee and embarrassment to the institution of the judiciary. And he could stare senators down. Perhaps, to moderate the institutional clash, he could move incrementally. He could, for example, begin with district court nominees, whose hearings remain cursory affairs in which nobody has much investment, and move from there to uncontroversial circuit court judges — leaving Supreme Court nominees and controversial circuit nominees for a later date. If he combined this move skillfully with close consultation with senators on the appointments themselves, senators might have enough investment in the individual nominees to waive the hearing, at least in low-profile cases.

The point is that the president has the power to push back, to object to the further development of the institution of live nominee testimony—and even to begin rolling it back.

And the chief justice—and the institutional judiciary in the form of the Judicial Conference—has the power to publicly back him, elevating the stance above partisan politics. It is not wholly clear to me that Roberts would endorse such a position. It is true that aspects of his own hearings troubled him deeply: the courtesy calls, the aggressive quality of the questioning, and the hearings' very length. "It's like running a marathon. It is an arduous process. And the people who were helping me made it clear; they said, 'Look, you're going to be sitting there for twelve hours. If you make a ten-second mistake, that's all anyone's going to know about,'" he recalled. "They don't have to be that long. The reason they are that long is because they are largely repetitive."

Still, perhaps surprisingly, Roberts valued other aspects. He made clear, for example, that he found the hearings "from a very personal point of view . . . to be . . . a very real moment. . . . I really felt this was it in the sense that my fifty years had come to this point both as an individual, since there are questions about you as an individual, [and] in terms of what [my] professional career had been. And I was particularly, given everything that had led up to it and gone before it, grateful to be here at that moment, saying: 'All right, I'm under oath, they can ask me anything and I get a chance to tell them what I really think about what judges do and about who I am.' And, you know, let's do it. That part of it was . . . in a real sense exhilarating."[21] As his quotation at the outset of this essay makes clear, Roberts retains an undying faith that the hearings process could function differently, in a more up-lifting fashion. Without the institutional support of the judiciary, though, any president would probably be too weak to take on the Senate.

Even with it, such a step would undoubtedly provoke a major

confrontation with the Senate, which would surely insist on the prerogative it has established—particularly if the opposition party controlled the body. It is far from clear which branch would prevail in the long run. For this reason, presidents might consider steps short of outright abolition of testimony as a kind of tactical concession to their reality, at least in the short term. To reduce the hearings' capacity for spectacle, presidents could push for private depositions by staff attorneys, with transcripts released to the public, rather than public interrogation by senators themselves. While such a scenario would still permit the grilling of the nominee, it would greatly reduce duplicative questioning and senatorial posturing and could enable more professional, sharper questioning that would bring out those limited areas about which nominees feel free to talk.

Short of any structural change, a president could simply insist that his nominees take a hard line in their responses to questions— that is, not respond to any questions about cases on which they have not written or spoken. Scalia's stance at his hearing seemed eccentric only against the background of the quasi-engagement of many other nominees. If all took the same position, sheer numbers would offer strength.

The broad point is that the institutional presidency needs to push to reestablish the unremarkable proposition that a nominee deserves consideration on the strength of his or her record. If that record does not justify confirmation—as was probably the case with Harriet Miers—nothing the nominee tells the Judiciary Committee ought to change that fact. By contrast, if a nominee's record justifies approval, the Senate should not need the charade of a multi-day interrogation to recognize its merit.

The flip side is that presidents need to stop pretending that the Senate has no legitimate room to consider a nominee's views in making its decision. A political culture that accepts wide judicial power cannot then contend that nominees' broad philosophical and jurisprudential positions have no bearing on their desirability. As I have sought to illustrate, this view misdescribes the way the Senate has long behaved and, indeed, is hard to justify in terms of how it *should* behave. As long as presidents fail to concede the Senate any legitimacy in considering a nominee's views, they position themselves badly to argue the real point: that it should not be obligating nominees to bare their souls to facilitate that ideological consideration.

This observation, too, carries consequences, for it implies the legitimacy of certain as-yet-untried tactics on the part of the Senate to assert itself in the process. The majority party, as I have suggested, could demand a measure of consultation as a condition of giving its consent for any nominee. It could even refuse to confirm a nominee not selected from a preapproved list of its own devising. Nothing in the Constitution forbids such an aggressive posture, which the Senate remains free to assume at any time. It has not done so, in large measure, because it has devoted all of its energy to aggrandizing its *confirmation* process, rather than applying pressure during the *nomination* phase of the appointments system. In other words, it has deployed its considerable and legitimate power against the wrong actors—the nominees—instead of deploying them against the presidency in such fashion as to maximally influence what sort of person presidents put forward in the first place. This, too, represents a historical error, one that senators—in an effort to maximize their own effect on the process—ought to endeavor to correct.

Deploying the Senate's power more properly would not, I concede, aid those liberals who today are concerned to combat the conservatism of President Bush's nominees. Then again, having control of neither of the institutions with a voice in the process, liberals *shouldn't* have substantial influence over it. Americans voted to give Republicans control both over the nominations and over the check on those nominations. It is not a fault but a virtue of the more targeted and effective senatorial assertions of power I envision that they would give the minority less opportunity to hijack the Senate's functioning as a body. On the other hand, imagine that Democrats take control over the Senate and that Justice John Paul Stevens resigns thereafter. A system under which the new Senate leadership would make clear and enforce its ideological expectations of the president's action, rather than wait passively while he chooses someone and then rely on a nationally televised interview process to try to discredit the choice, offers a far more promising avenue for the protection of liberal values.

These are angry times, but they are not by any means the first period of particular partisan polarization in American history—or even, by historical standards, an especially intense one. Indeed, prior periods of partisan division offer an alternative model for how we might handle confirmations. Throughout most of the nineteenth century, the Senate was dramatically more aggressive than it is today in its willingness to reject Supreme Court nominations, either because of political difference with the nominees or because of political opposition to the nominating president. The Senate, for example, rejected four different individuals nominated for the Supreme Court by President John Tyler alone, one of them twice. It rejected George Washington's nomination of John Rutledge to be chief justice in 1795 for his criticisms of the Jay Treaty. It initially rejected Chief Justice Roger Taney because of his assistance to President Andrew Jackson as Treasury secretary in removing federal money from the Bank of the United States. It rejected one particularly worthy nominee, Ebenezer Hoar, for having advanced civil service reform.[22] The Senate, in other words, had no trouble making its ideological voice heard and saying no to nominees who did not suit the majority's taste. Presidents did not treat such aggressiveness as an impropriety. And senators, for their part, understood better than they do today that focusing their institution's power on pressuring the nominator, not on interrogating the nominee, made for both a more effective and a more civilized deployment of that power.

This, it seems to me, is the direction in which we need to push the process now. It is quite unreasonable to expect that the confirmation of judges will magically take place free of political considerations; the Framers of the Constitution designed a system that involved the two political branches of government. It is not, however, unreasonable at all to expect the politics surrounding nominations to function more rationally, to expect the political branches to pursue their goals at once more effectively and with greater regard for the judicial function and—we might even hope—for the individuals who aspire to serve as judges. Neither the Senate nor the institutional presidency will do so on its own. Each, however, does have the power to push the other in the right direction if it chooses to exercise that power, instead of behaving as it does now.

This will not "fix" a "broken" system.[23] "Broken," in fact, is really the wrong word for a process that, ugliness and all, gets enough people confirmed that the judiciary only occasionally has workforce shortages. The better way to think about the system is as a series of tools, each being employed for a task somewhat remote from its purpose. One could use an automobile engine to heat a house, for example, but it would produce inefficient heating at great expense and high environmental impact and with the constant danger of carbon monoxide poisoning or some other hazard. Something similar is taking place here. Our constitutional instruments are not so inapt that they do not work at all, but we have configured them badly enough that they serve our purposes with remarkable inefficiency, high collateral consequences, and needlessly elevated danger of far greater consequences.

I no longer believe, with the chief justice, that the confirmation process could function as some kind of "uplifting, educational, informative discussion about . . . the role of the courts [or] the appropriate judicial philosophy." Indeed, I wish nothing more strenuously for the process than that it would stop trying—that it would narrow its ambitions, state them more honestly, and pursue them more cleanly. A political check need not harbor delusions of grandeur.

ACKNOWLEDGMENTS

Developing the argument contained in this book required several years of thought and reporting. But I wrote down the text itself in only a few short weeks, during a brief leave from the *Washington Post* in 2006. Because of the speed with which I wrote it, I relied particularly heavily on the assistance of several people for whom the following thanks can serve only as the weakest sort of repayment. Peter Berkowitz and Tod Lindberg of the Hoover Institution were kind enough to invite me to write the book and treated serial delays—the result of the seemingly endless Supreme Court nominations of 2005 and the early part of this year—with gracious tolerance. I am grateful to Tod for his unstinting support of the project. Several of the key arguments that appear in these pages were forged and refined in the crucible of dinner-table conversations with Peter over the past few years. His editorial wisdom pervades, perhaps invisibly, much of the work. Rachel Abrams, also of Hoover, performed a helpful early edit. The manuscript benefited enormously from the timely and insightful comments of Jack Goldsmith, Jeffrey Rosen, David Tell, Jonathan Rauch, and Charles Lane—all of whom forced me to address questions I had initially elided or to tighten aspects of my argument.

The specific research that ultimately led to this book began with a short article for the *Atlantic Monthly*, which has, in general, given my work a wonderful platform. My repeated citations to their books in footnotes somehow do not account in full for my intellectual debt to Henry J. Abraham and John Anthony Maltese, whose work has dramatically conditioned my own understanding of the history of Supreme Court nominations and confirmations. I have also benefited from countless conversations over the past decade with sitting judges and judicial nominees about the confirmation process; while I am not at liberty to name these people or detail the conversations, the insights I gleaned from them pervade every sentence I have written. My wife, Tamara Cofman Wittes, as she always does, served as a critical sounding-board for ideas good and bad.

I honestly don't know how I would have finished this project without the research assistance of Rebecca Rosen, who spent a month combing through the Library of Congress for records of old nominations. Autumn Brewington saved me from numerous embarrassing errors—as she and her colleagues on the editorial page copy desk so often do—and polished the manuscript with a thoughtful and rigorous copy-editing job. The staff at the Politics & Prose coffee shop, where I wrote most of the book, deserves a word of thanks as well for their warmth and friendliness, good coffee, and free Wi-Fi.

Finally, I could not have written this book had I not had the privilege these past nine years of writing editorials for the *Washington Post*, a newspaper for which taking a position of principle still means something. I am deeply indebted to Fred Hiatt and the extraordinary group of colleagues with whom I sit around a table each morning. If there exists another institution in the country so consistently committed to debating and evaluating judicial nominees on their merits and uninflected by partisan politics, I am unaware of it. I could never have undertaken my own work on this subject without the support, insightful observations, spirited arguments, occasional disagreements, and uniform commitment to getting the right answer of my colleagues on the *Post's* editorial page. To them I consequently dedicate this book.

NOTES

■

Chapter 1

1. The court's lore on this subject, Roberts emphasized, is of uncertain historical provenance.
2. The ad was run by NARAL Pro-Choice America. FactCheck.org, a nonpartisan watchdog Web site devoted to accuracy in political discourse, published a substantial critique of it. The critique, which includes the ad's full written text and video, can be found at http://www.factcheck.org/article340.html, as can NARAL's defense of its ad.
3. At one point, for example, reporters from the *New York Times* looked into the circumstances of Roberts's adoption of his two children. See Todd J. Gillman, "Hutchison: Roberts line crossed; She blasts look into nominee's adoptions; paper calls it routine," *Dallas Morning News*, August 6, 2005, 19A.
4. John G. Roberts Jr., interview with the author, January 13, 2006.
5. For a typical example of conservative anxiety, see Robert Bork, "American Conservatism: The Soul of the Law," *Wall Street Journal*, January 20, 2003, A14. Bork writes, seamlessly blending decades-old jurisprudence with modern decisions, "The Supreme Court has created a more permissive abortion regime than any state had enacted; prohibited any exercise or symbol of religion touching even remotely upon government; made the death penalty extremely

difficult to impose and execute; disabled states from suppressing pornography; catered to the feminist agenda, including outlawing state all-male military schools; created a labyrinth of procedures making criminal prosecutions ever more difficult; used racial classifications to exclude children from their neighborhood public schools; perverted the political process by upholding campaign finance limits that shift political power to incumbents, journalists, and labor unions; licensed the advocacy of violence and law violation; and protected as free speech computer-generated child pornography. These decisions are activist, i.e., not plausibly related to the actual Constitution."

6. Like any rule, this one has its exceptions. The Court has famously extended the right to privacy to strike down state sodomy laws, for example. See *Lawrence v. Texas*, 539 U.S. 558 (2003). It has also expanded protections in capital cases under the Eighth Amendment. See *Atkins v. Virginia*, 536 U.S. 304 (2002) and *Roper v. Simmons*, 543 U.S. 551 (2005). For all the anger such cases have caused in conservative circles, however, they do not represent the Court's norm of business these days.

7. For a typical example of liberal anxiety, see Cass R. Sunstein, *Radicals in Robes: Why Extreme Right-Wing Courts Are Wrong for America* (New York: Basic Books, 2005), 8: "By 2005, the Constitution was starting to look a bit more like it did in 1920. The powers of the national government were being limited, the rights of criminal defendants were scaled back, the Constitution offered less to members of minority groups, and the rights of private property owners were being expanded. In 2005, the Constitution did not look exactly as Richard Nixon or Ronald Reagan envisioned it. But it made major moves in their direction."

8. Gallup's trend line both on confidence in the Court and on its political orientation can be found at: http://poll.gallup.com/content/default.aspx?ci=4732 (subscription required).

9. See, for example, Editorial, "Not a Campaign," *Washington Post*, July 3, 2005, B6: "Seconds After President Bush announces his choice to replace Supreme Court Justice Sandra Day O'Connor — whenever that happens and whoever the nominee is — liberal interest groups will release a blast of e-mails promising a 'rollback' of American liberties if the person is confirmed. Conservative groups, at the same moment, will blitz with e-mails proclaiming the nominee a modern John Marshall. Ads will appear on television. Journalists will

be hit with distorted 'reports' attacking or defending the nominee's 'record,' as groups release their opposition research or their defensive spin. Both camps, in short, will unleash the huge sums they have raised in what will be, for all intents and purposes, a political campaign—a political campaign, unfortunately, for an office that is meant to be not merely apolitical but actively insulated from politics."

10. I know Estrada's views on *U.S. v. Lopez*, 514 U.S. 549 (1995) and its progeny from numerous private conversations with him. Estrada, I should disclose, has become a personal friend in the years since his withdrawal as a nominee.

11. 28 U.S.C. § 458 then read: "No person shall be appointed to or employed in any office or duty in any court who is related by affinity or consanguinity within the degree of first cousin to any justice or judge of such court." The Justice Department's Office of Legal Counsel determined that this law, which dates originally from the nineteenth century, was never intended to apply to presidential appointment of judges actually to serve on the courts, only to court staff. Other close relatives had served on courts together in the past, including the legendary cousins Learned and Augustus Hand. Indeed, any reading applying it to presidential appointment of judges would raise a serious constitutional problem to the extent that it encumbered the president's power to appoint a judge and the Senate's power to consent to the appointment. Assistant Attorney General Walter Dellinger's memorandum "Application of 28 U.S.C. § 458 to Presidential Appointments of Federal Judges," dated December 18, 1995, can be found at http://www.usdoj.gov/olc/willy.fin.32.htm.

12. See Helen Dewar and Joan Biskupic, "Hatch Vows Action on Stalled 9th Circuit Nomination," *Washington Post*, May 8, 1998, A6. Clinton acceded to Gorton's choice of Barbara Durham, chief justice of Washington's Supreme Court, but Durham had her name withdrawn after her nomination, citing her husband's health problems. Shortly thereafter, she resigned from the state court amid health problems of her own and died in 2002. The seat Gorton sought for her went to Richard Tallman. Congress, in conjunction with Fletcher's confirmation, amended 28 U.S.C. § 458 to make clear that "No person may be appointed to the position of judge of a court exercising judicial power under article III of the United States Constitution (other than the Supreme Court) who is related by affinity or consanguinity within the degree of first cousin to any

judge who is a member of the same court." The application to judges is almost surely unconstitutional.

13. In his note to the group's head, James C. Dobson, Alito wrote: "This is just a short note to express my heartfelt thanks to you and the entire staff of Focus on the Family for your help and support during the past few challenging months. I would also greatly appreciate it if you would convey my appreciation to the good people from all parts of the country who wrote to tell me that they were praying for me and for my family during this period. As I said when I spoke at my formal investiture at the White House last week, the prayers of so many people from around the country were a palpable and powerful force.

"As long as I serve on the Supreme Court I will keep in mind the trust that has been placed in me. I hope that we will have the opportunity to meet personally at some point in the future. In the meantime my entire family and I hope that you and the Focus on the Family staff know how much we appreciate all that you have done." See Alan Cooperman, "Thanks From Alito," *Washington Post*, March 2, 2006, A19.

14. *Brown v. Board of Education*, 347 U.S. 483 (1954).

15. *Roe v. Wade*, 410 U.S. 113 (1973).

16. See United States Constitution, Article II, Section 2.

Chapter 2

1. Lee Epstein and Jeffrey A. Segal, *Advice and Consent: The Politics of Judicial Appointments* (Oxford: Oxford University Press, 2005), 4.

2. Ibid., 2–3.

3. Ibid., 144.

4. Richard A. Posner, "The Supreme Court 2004 Term — Foreword: A Political Court," *Harvard Law Review 119*, No. 31 (2005): 48–49.

5. Ibid., 46.

6. Michael Comiskey, *Seeking Justices: The Judging of Supreme Court Nominees* (Lawrence: University Press of Kansas, 2004), 193–194.

7. For the Judiciary Committee's consideration of Stone's nomination, see *Report of Proceedings: Hearing held before Subcommittee of the Committee on the Judiciary — Stone Nomination*, 77th Cong., 1st sess., 1941, SJ-T20. The transcript is two pages long. No witness wished to speak concerning Stone. For the committee's consideration of Vinson's nomination, which is only marginally more substantial, see *Hearing held before Subcommittee of the Committee on*

the Judiciary: Nomination of Fred M. Vinson, 79th Cong., 2d sess., 1946, SJ-T18.

8. Epstein and Segal, *Advice and Consent*, 2–4.

9. For an excellent discussion of this shift, see Nancy Scherer, *Scoring Points: Politicians, Activists, and the Lower Federal Court Appointment Process* (Stanford: Stanford University Press, 2005).

10. According to data published by the *New York Times* on November 15, 2003, in a graphic on page A10 entitled "Confirmations Over the Long Haul," during the Roosevelt administration, the Senate failed to confirm 2 percent of the president's lower-court nominees. During the administrations of George H.W. Bush and Bill Clinton and through the first two years of George W. Bush's administration, the Senate failed to confirm nearly 25 percent of lower-court nominees. *Scoring Points* contains a useful, brief discussion of this and related data on pages 1–4.

11. Stephen B. Presser, "The Role of the Senate in Judicial Confirmations," May 8, 2003, http://www.fed-soc.org/Publications/hot topics/may03.pdf. Presser's article appears on the Web site of the Federalist Society as part of "An Exchange on the Judicial Confirmation Process."

12. Robert H. Bork, "Their Will Be Done," *Wall Street Journal*, July 5, 2005, A20.

13. See, for example, Editorial, "The Return of 'Borking,'" *Wall Street Journal*, May 8, 2001, A26. The editorial expresses shock at Democratic senators' aggressive use early in the Bush administration of the Judiciary Committee's "blue slips," which allow senators to block consideration of nominees to courts in their states, and dismisses similar Republican moves during the Clinton years. The *Journal*'s editorial writers are surely less naïve about the stalling of President Clinton's nominees than this editorial suggests, having egged it on at times themselves. See, for example, Editorial, "A GOP Judicial Debacle?" *Wall Street Journal*, May 16, 2000, A26, which blasted the Judiciary Committee's then-chairman, Orrin Hatch, for holding a hearing for D.C. Circuit nominee Allen Snyder "only months before an election [Republicans] might even win." Snyder never received a vote.

14. To cite only one example both of conservative playing down of excesses and of justifying them as defensive, Senator Jeff Sessions has been one of the most vociferous objectors to Democratic uses of the filibuster and has loudly denied any comparable Republican

tactics. At the time of the agreement to limit use of the filibuster, for example, he insisted that he had voted to give up-or-down votes on the Senate floor to Marsha Berzon and Richard Paez—two of Clinton's "very activist judge nominees for the Ninth Circuit Court of Appeals," despite strongly opposing them. See *Congressional Record*, 109th Cong., 1st sess., May 23, 2005. Vol. 151, no. 69, S5812–5813. This was true but entirely incomplete. Sessions had waged a long campaign to stall both nominations, which he had helped hold up for years. And he made no bones about why. Paez, he said on March 9, 2000, "has been held up for a number of years for reasons that have been discussed in some detail. He has stated, as a State judge, a philosophy of judging that is the absolute epitome of judicial activism. He said that when a legislative body doesn't act, it is the responsibility of the judge, or the judiciary, to act and fill the void." See *Congressional Record*, 106th Cong., 2d sess., March 9, 2000. Vol. 146, no. 26, S1346. Even after the Senate invoked cloture, Sessions wasn't finished. He moved to indefinitely postpone a vote on Paez, a motion that was defeated on a 67–31 vote. See page S1368.

15. Scalia's March 14 speech at the Woodrow Wilson International Center for Scholars is summarized on the center's Web site at http://www.wilsoncenter.org/index.cfm?fuseaction=events.event_su mmary&event_id=114173. A transcript is available at http://www .cfif.org/htdocs/legal_issues/legal_updates/us_supreme_court/scalia -constitutional-speech.htm.

16. John R. Lott Jr., "Confirmation Trials: Causes and Consequences of Judicial Selection Battles," unpublished manuscript.

17. Ibid., 8.

18. Ibid., 17.

19. Ibid., 24.

20. Ibid., 9.

21. *Colegrove v. Green*, 328 U.S. 549 (1946).

22. The Senate confirmed Burger barely two weeks after receiving his nomination in 1969 following a brief hearing.

23. Bork, *Wall Street Journal*, "Their Will Be Done."

24. George F. Will, "Damaging 'Deference,'" *Washington Post*, June 24, 2005, A31.

25. George F. Will, "The Value of 'Activism,'" *Washington Post*, September 1, 2005, A29.

26. Herman Schwartz, *Right Wing Justice: The Conservative Campaign to Take Over the Courts* (New York: Nation Books, 2004), 40.
27. Ibid, 42.
28. Sunstein, *Radicals in Robes*, 9–13.
29. Ibid., 14.
30. Cass Sunstein, "The Right-Wing Assault," *American Prospect*, March 1, 2003, http://www.prospect.org/web/page.ww?section=root&name=ViewPrint&articleId=6725.
31. Sunstein, *Radicals in Robes*, 15.
32. Ibid., 14.
33. See Henry J. Abraham, *Justices, Presidents, and Senators: A History of the U.S. Supreme Court Appointments from Washington to Clinton* (Lanham: Rowman & Littlefield Publishers, Inc., 1999), 182. Abraham describes Truman's four Supreme Court nominees as "his political, professional, and personal friends; he understood them; he liked them; he liked their politics. Loyal to a fault, he wanted to reward them, and he did—to Truman, loyalty was far more significant than ideology."
34. Ibid., 9–10.
35. For a useful account of the deterioration of the process during the Reagan years, see *Scoring Points*, Chapter 5. For a more polemical account, see *Right Wing Justice*, Chapter 2.
36. See Jeffrey Rosen, "The Unregulated Offensive," *New York Times Magazine*, April 17, 2005, 42.
37. Ken Foskett, *Judging Thomas: The Life and Times of Clarence Thomas* (New York: Perennial, 2005), 281–282. Foskett quotes Justice Scalia as saying of Thomas, "He does not believe in *stare decisis*, period." Scalia goes on to say, "If a constitutional line of authority is wrong, he would say let's get it right. I wouldn't do that."
38. The high court voted 7–2 in *Dickerson v. U.S.*, 530 U.S. 428 (2000), to reaffirm the vitality of *Miranda v. Arizona*, 384 U.S. 436 (1966), whose original majority consisted of only five votes.
39. Roberts's testimony concerning the right to privacy can be found at http://www.washingtonpost.com/wp-dyn/content/article/2005/09/13/AR2005091300876.html. Alito's can be found at http://www.washingtonpost.com/wp-dyn/content/article/2006/01/10/AR2006011000781.html.
40. For my views on this subject, see Benjamin Wittes, "The Hapless Toad," *Atlantic Monthly*, May 1, 2005, 48.

41. For my views on this subject, see Benjamin Wittes, "Letting Go of *Roe*," *Atlantic Monthly*, January 1, 2005, 48.

42. See *Hopwood v. Texas*, 78 F.3d 932 (5th Cir. 1996).

43. For a good discussion of the troubling distortions of Bork's record and the distinctions between those distortions and legitimate criticism, see Stephen L. Carter, *The Confirmation Mess: Cleaning Up the Federal Appointments Process* (New York: Basic Books, 1994), 45–50.

44. See *Hearings Before the Committee on the Judiciary United States Senate: Confirmation Hearings on Federal Appointments*, 107th Cong., 2d sess., 2002, Senate Hearing 107–584, Part 5, 779–780, 802–803, 805–808, 811–815, 819–821. Two anonymous sources had told the *Nation* magazine that Estrada had attempted to screen out liberals in assisting Justice Anthony Kennedy—for whom he had clerked—select new clerks. See Jack Newfield, "The Right's Judicial Juggernaut," *Nation*, October 7, 2002, 11.

45. Sunstein himself has played a role on this point. At Estrada's hearing, Senator Schumer unveiled as-yet-unpublished data Sunstein had provided him in support of his contention that the ideology of judges plays a significant role in the votes they cast. *Estrada Hearing*, 765. Earlier, Sunstein also spoke at a private retreat for Democratic senators as part of an effort early in the Bush administration to develop what the *New York Times* called "a unified party strategy to combat the White House on judicial nominees." See Neil A. Lewis, "Democrats Readying for Judicial Fight," *New York Times*, May 1, 2001, 19.

46. Anthony Lewis, "Reagan and the Court," *New York Times*, October 9, 1980, 35.

47. Carter, *The Confirmation Mess*, ix.

48. Ibid., 16.

49. Ibid., 95.

50. Ibid., 142–143.

51. Ibid., 205–206.

52. For a few recent examples, see Editorial, "Nuclear Freeze," *Washington Post*, April 8, 2005, A24; Editorial, "A New Start on Courts," *Washington Post*, November 10, 2004, A26; Editorial, "Blah, Blah, Blah," *Washington Post*, November 12, 2003, A22; Editorial, "Second Chance on Judges," *Washington Post*, November 8, 2002, A30; Editorial, "President Bush and Judges," *Washington Post*, January 29, 2001, A18.

53. Carter, *The Confirmation Mess*, 206.

Chapter 3

1. For data on Presidents Truman through Ford see Congressional Research Service Report RL32122, *Judicial Nomination Statistics: U.S. District and Circuit Courts, 1945–1976*, by Mitchel A. Sollenberger, October 22, 2003, Table 2. For data on President Carter, see Congressional Research Service Report RL31635, *Judicial Nomination Statistics: U.S. District and Circuit Courts, 1977–2003*, by Denis Steven Rutkus and Mitchel A. Sollenberger, February 23, 2004, Table 2.

2. For data on Presidents Truman through Ford see CRS Report RL32122, Table 7. For data on President Carter, see CRS Report RL31635, Table 8.

3. CRS Report RL31635, Table 8.

4. Congressional Research Service Report RL31868, *U.S. Circuit and District Court Nominations by George W. Bush during the 107th–109th Congresses*, by Denis Steven Rutkus and Maureen Bearden, May 24, 2006.

5. Ibid., 30–33.

6. Lott, *Confirmation Trials*, 35–38. See Figures 3-1 and 3-2.

7. CRS Report RL31868, Table 3.

8. Lott, *Confirmation Trials*, 38. See Figure 3-2.

9. Ibid., 50.

10. For my earlier formulation of this problem, see Benjamin Wittes, "Too Smart to Be a Judge," *Washington Post*, June 11, 2002, A25.

11. Wilkinson made these remarks at a panel discussion on judicial nominations at the American Academy of Arts and Sciences on March 21, 2002.

12. See Congressional Research Service Report RL33225, *Supreme Court Nominations, 1789–2005: Actions by the Senate, the Judiciary Committee, and the President*, by Denis Steven Rutkus and Maureen Bearden, January 5, 2006, Table 1. See also *Confirmation Trials*, 13, Figure 2-1.

13. Comiskey, *Seeking Justices*, 12.

14. For a good account of Stone's nomination, see Alpheus Thomas Mason, *Harlan Fiske Stone: Pillar of the Law* (New York: Viking Press, 1956), 568–574.

15. *Congressional Record*, 77th Cong., 1st sess., June 27, 1941. Vol. 87, part 5, 5618–5619.

16. Article II, Section 2, Clause 3 of the Constitution gives the president the power "to fill up all Vacancies that may happen during the Recess of the Senate, by granting Commissions which shall expire at the End of their next Session." Eisenhower's confidence that Warren would not attract controversy proved premature. Warren's confirmation by the Senate got held up in a patronage dispute with a powerful member of the Judiciary Committee, William Langer of North Dakota, who—as Henry Abraham recounts—"had then begun his prolonged six-year campaign of opposing any and all nominees to the Court until someone from his home state (which had never been so honored) received an appointment. (He went to his grave in 1959, his hopes still unrealized—as they are to this day.)" See *Justices, Presidents, and Senators*, 194. Placed on the bench on October 2, 1953, he did not receive the permanent nod from the Senate until March 1, 1954.

17. Clinton drew fire for his recess appointment of Roger Gregory to the U.S. Court of Appeals for the Fourth Circuit shortly before he left office. Bush attracted criticism for his recess appointments of William Pryor to the Eleventh Circuit and Charles Pickering to the Fifth Circuit.

18. By the time Eisenhower used the recess appointment power with Stewart, it provoked some negative reaction among senators inclined to oppose Stewart anyway. See Senate Committee on the Judiciary, *Nomination of Potter Stewart*, 86th Cong., 1st sess., 1959, Executive Report No. 2, 2–10.

19. CRS Report RL33225, Table 1.

20. Ibid.

21. I know of this incident as a result of numerous conversations with Estrada.

22. John Anthony Maltese, *The Selling of Supreme Court Nominees* (Baltimore: The Johns Hopkins University Press, 1995), Chapter 2.

23. Abraham, *Justices, Presidents, and Senators*, 135.

24. Testimony of Clifford Thorne, *Hearings before the Senate Subcommittee of the Committee on the Judiciary: The Nomination of Louis D. Brandeis to be an Associate Justice of the Supreme Court of the United States*, 64th Cong., 1st sess., 1916, SJ-1, 8.

25. Ibid. Testimony of Albert E. Pillsbury, 653.

26. Abraham, *Justices, Presidents, and Senators*, 136.

27. Editorial, "An Unfit Appointment," *Los Angeles Times*, January 30, 1916, II4.

28. Editorial, "The Brandeis Nomination," *New York Times*, May 25, 1916, 12.

29. Maltese, *The Selling of Supreme Court Nominees*, 97.

30. Ibid., 52.

31. Ibid., 52–53.

32. Abraham, *Justices, Presidents, and Senators*, 150–151.

33. *Congressional Record*, 71st Cong., 2d sess., February 10, 1930. Vol. 72, part 3, 3373.

34. Ibid., 3449, February 11, 1930.

35. Ibid., 3510–3511, February 12, 1930.

36. For an excellent account of Parker's defeat, see *The Selling of Supreme Court Nominees*, Chapter 4.

37. *International Organization United Mine Workers of America v. Red Jacket Consolidated Coal & Coke Co.*, 18 F.2d 839 (4th Cir. 1927).

38. Testimony of William Green, *Hearing before the Senate Subcommittee of the Committee on the Judiciary on the Confirmation of Hon. John J. Parker to be an Associate Justice of the Supreme Court of the United States*, 71st Cong., 2d sess., 1930, S331-12, 55.

39. *Hitchman Coal & Coke Co. v. Mitchell*, 245 U.S. 229 (1916).

40. The text of Parker's letter is printed in *Congressional Record*, 71st Cong., 2d sess., April 28, 1930. Vol. 72, part 7, 7793–7794.

41. White's testimony, including the quotation from Parker's speech, can be found in the *Parker Hearing* transcript on pages 74–79.

42. Parker letter.

43. Abraham, *Justices, Presidents, and Senators*, 151.

44. Ibid., 31. Abraham cites two, including *Rice v. Elmore*, 165 F.2d 387 (4th Cir. 1947), in which Parker wrote an opinion affirming an injunction that barred South Carolina from preventing qualified blacks from voting in Democratic primary elections—a case brought by Thurgood Marshall. Wrote Parker, "the denial to the Negro of the right to participate in the primary denies him all effective voice in the government of his country. There can be no question that such denial amounts to a denial of the constitutional rights of the Negro; and we think it equally clear that those who participate in the denial are exercising state power to that end, since the primary is used in connection with the general election in the selection of state officers." Parker also signed a key implementing decision for

one of the school desegregation cases that went to the Supreme Court with *Brown*, a South Carolina case called *Briggs v. Elliott*, 132 F. Supp 776 (District of South Carolina 1955), though he had, prior to *Brown*, upheld segregated public schools in that state under the "separate but equal" doctrine.

45. Maltese, *The Selling of Supreme Court Nominees*, 69.

46. *Congressional Record*, 71st Cong., 2d sess., April 28, 1930. Vol. 72, part 8, 7930.

47. Ibid., 7939.

48. Parker actually telegrammed the Judiciary Committee to communicate his willingness to testify concerning the matters that ultimately led to his defeat. But the committee voted down the idea and reported the nomination unfavorably without hearing from him. See "Committee, 10 to 6, Rejects Parker," *New York Times*, April 22, 1930, 1.

49. See *Justices, Presidents, and Senators*, 197–198, concerning Harlan and 205 concerning Stewart.

50. See *The Confirmation Mess*, 1–2, 75–77.

51. *Congressional Record*, 90th Cong., 2d sess., June 26, 1968. Vol. 114, part 14, 18874.

52. Abraham, *Justices, Presidents, and Senators*, 10. A thorough account of the Haynsworth nomination can be found in *The Selling of Supreme Court Nominees*, Chapter 5.

53. Testimony of George Meany, *Hearings Before The Committee on the Judiciary United States Senate: Nomination of Clement F. Haynsworth, Jr., of South Carolina, to be Associate Justice of the Supreme Court of the United States*, 91st Cong., 1st sess., 1969, S1953-12, 163.

54. Ibid., 423–424. Testimony of Legislative Director Clarence Mitchell, reading a prepared statement of organization co-founder Roy Wilkins.

55. *Congressional Record*, 91st Cong., 1st sess., October 2, 1969. Vol. 115, part 21, 28211.

56. Abraham, *Justices, Presidents, and Senators*, 11–13.

57. Lott, *Confirmation Trials*, 12–13.

58. Charles L. Black, Jr., "A Note on Senatorial Consideration of Supreme Court Nominees," Yale Law Journal 79 (1970):657.

59. Scherer, *Scoring Points*, 28.

60. William H. Rehnquist, *All the Laws but One: Civil Liberties in War-*

time (New York: Alfred A. Knopf, 1998), 16. The historical authenticity of this quotation is apparently open to question. For its history, see Matthew J. Franck, "What Did Lincoln Say? The 16th President and SCOTUS Nominees," *National Review Online*, July 6, 2005, http:// www.nationalreview.com/comment/franck200507060812.asp. For present purposes, however, it matters little if the quotation is authentic or if it is an apocryphal placing of one of the political culture's taboos in the mouth of one of its great heroes. Either way, it reflects the norm that the politician who wished for certainty had to get it by some means other than asking the question.

61. For a fuller account of the circumstances of the nomination, see *Harlan Fiske Stone: Pillar of the Law*, Chapter 12. See also *The Selling of Supreme Court Nominees*, 99–101.

62. If a full transcript of this hearing survives, I have been unable to identify a copy. The *Washington Post*, however, published extended excerpts from the hearing at the time it took place. See "Text of Principal Points in Attorney General's Testimony," *Washington Post*, January 29, 1925, 8; "Stone's Statement to the Committee," *Washington Post*, January 29, 1925, 9.

63. Albert W. Fox, "Stone Tells Senate Committee He Assumes Full Responsibility for Pressing New Wheeler Case," *Washington Post*, January 29, 1925, 1.

64. Editorial, "Thank God for a MAN!" *Washington Post*, January 29, 1925, 6.

65. An account of Frankfurter's confirmation can be found in *The Selling of Supreme Court Nominees*, 104–107.

66. *Hearings Before a Subcommittee of the Committee on the Judiciary United States Senate on the Nomination of Felix Frankfurter to be an Associate Justice of the Supreme Court*, 76th Cong., 1st sess., 1939, S578-7, 107–108.

67. Ibid., 108–113, 123–124.

68. Ibid., 125–128.

69. See *Hearings Before a Subcommittee of the Committee on the Judiciary United States Senate: Nomination of Robert H. Jackson to be an Associate Justice of the Supreme Court*, 77th Cong., 1st sess., 1941, S667-9, 56–69.

70. *Minutes Subcommittee, Judiciary Committee: Nomination of Frank Murphy to be Associate Justice, Sup. Ct.*, 76th Cong., 2d sess., 1940. Published in *The Supreme Court of the United States: Hearings and Reports on Successful and Unsuccessful Nominations of Supreme*

Court Justices by the Senate Judiciary Committee, 1916–1975, vol. 4.

71. For a full account of Harlan's nomination, see Tinsley E. Yarbrough, *John Marshall Harlan: Great Dissenter of the Warren Court* (Oxford: Oxford University Press, 1992), 86–113.

72. *Hearings Before the Committee on the Judiciary United States Senate: Nomination of John Marshall Harlan of New York to be Associate Justice of the Supreme Court of the United States*, 84th Cong., 1st sess., 1955, S1112-13, 129–182.

73. For more information on the controversy over the so-called Bricker Amendment, see Duane Tananbaum, *The Bricker Amendment Controversy: A Test of Eisenhower's Political Leadership* (Ithaca: Cornell University Press, 1988). See also Natalie Hevener Kaufman, *Human Rights Treaties and the Senate: A History of Opposition* (Chapel Hill: University of North Carolina Press, 1990), Chapter 4.

74. *Congressional Record*, 84th Cong., 1st sess., March 16, 1955. Vol. 101, part 3, 3013.

75. Editorial, "Confirmation At Last," *Washington Post and Times Herald*, March 18, 1955, 20.

76. See *Rice v. Sioux City Memorial Park Cemetery, Inc.*, 349 U.S. 70 (1955).

77. *Harlan Hearings*, 140–141.

78. Yarbrough, *John Marshall Harlan: Great Dissenter of the Warren Court*, 98–99.

79. Eastland's speech can be found in *Congressional Record*, 84th Cong., 1st sess., March 16, 1955. Vol. 101, part 3, 3012–3013. Harlan's comment can be found in *Harlan Hearings*, 138.

80. Editorial, "Dangerous Nonsense," *New York Times*, February 27, 1955, E8.

81. Editorial, "Niggling Over Harlan," *Washington Post*, March 2, 1955, 12.

82. Yarbrough, *John Marshall Harlan: Great Dissenter of the Warren Court*, 112.

83. *Hearings Before the Committee on the Judiciary United States Senate: Nomination of William Joseph Brennan, Junior, of New Jersey, to be Associate Justice of the Supreme Court of the United States*, 85th Cong., 1st sess., 1957, S1252-3, 17–22.

84. Ibid., 22–29.

85. Ibid., 17.

86. Kim Isaac Eisler, *A Justice for All: William J. Brennan, Jr., and the Decisions that Transformed America* (New York: Simon & Schuster, 1993), 117.

87. *Brennan Hearings*, 36–38.

88. See Footnote 11 in *Brown v. Board of Education*, 347 U.S. 483 (1954).

89. *Hearing Before the Committee on the Judiciary United States Senate: Nomination of Charles E. Whittaker, of Missouri, to be Associate Justice of the Supreme Court of the United States*, 85th Cong., 1st sess., 1957, S1252-2, 32–34.

90. *Hearing Before the Committee on the Judiciary United States Senate: Nomination of Byron R. White, of Colorado, to be Associate Justice of the Supreme Court of the United States*, 87th Cong., 2d sess., 1962, S1491-5, 22–26.

91. *Hearings Before the Committee on the Judiciary United States Senate: Nomination of Arthur J. Goldberg, of Illinois, to be Associate Justice of the Supreme Court of the United States*, 87th Cong., 2d sess., 1962, S1532-4, 23–32.

92. *Hearing Before the Committee on the Judiciary United States Senate: Nomination of Abe Fortas, of Tennessee, to be an Associate Justice of the Supreme Court of the United States*, 89th Cong., 1st sess., 1965, S1700-4, 41–44.

93. Ibid., 51–55

94. *Stewart Nomination*, 20–21, 26.

95. Ibid., 15–16.

96. Ibid., 17–18.

97. Ibid., 33–34.

98. Ibid., 41–60.

99. Editorial, "Badgering Judges," *Washington Post and Times Herald*, April 11, 1959, A8.

100. *Stewart Nomination*, 63–64.

101. Abraham, *Justices, Presidents, and Senators*, 221.

102. *Hearings Before the Committee on the Judiciary United States Senate: Nomination of Thurgood Marshall, of New York, to be an Associate Justice of the Supreme Court of the United States*, 90th Cong., 1st sess., 1967, S1826-3, 161.

103. Thurmond's bizarre interrogation can be found in *Marshall Hearings*, 161–176.

104. Ibid. The subject comes up repeatedly, 9–60. See also pages 88–91.

105. Ibid., 66–74. The cases discussed included *South Carolina v. Katzenbach*, 383 U.S. 301 (1966) and *Katzenbach v. Morgan*, 384 U.S. 641 (1966).
106. *Marshall Hearings*, 93–106.
107. Ibid., 14.
108. Ibid., 54.
109. Ibid., 179.
110. Carter, *The Confirmation Mess*, 65.
111. *Haynsworth Hearings*, 75–76.
112. See William H. Rehnquist, "The Making of a Supreme Court Justice," Harvard Law Record 29 (October 8, 1959): 7. Wrote the future chief justice, "It is high time that those critical of the present Court recognize with the late Charles Evans Hughes that for one hundred seventy-five years the constitution has been what the judges say it is. If greater judicial self-restraint is desired, or a different interpretation of the phrases 'due process of law' or 'equal protection of the laws', then men sympathetic to such desires must sit upon the high court. The only way for the Senate to learn of these sympathies is to 'inquire of men on their way to the Supreme Court something of their views on these questions.'"
113. *Hearings Before the Committee on the Judiciary United States Senate: Nominations of William H. Rehnquist, of Arizona, and Lewis F. Powell, Jr., of Virginia, to be Associate Justices of the Supreme Court of the United States*, 92nd Cong., 1st sess., 1971, 26.
114. Ibid., 33–34.
115. Ibid., 39.
116. Ibid., 51.
117. Ibid., 56. See also questioning by Sen. Bayh, 69–70.
118. Ibid., 62–63.
119. Ibid., 163.
120. Ibid., 164.
121. Ibid., 77.
122. Ibid., 157.
123. See, to cite two almost random examples, *Hearing Before a Subcommittee of the Committee on the Judiciary United States Senate: Nomination of Claude C. McColloch to be Judge of the United States District Court for the District of Oregon*, 75th Cong., 1st sess., 1937, S547-13; *Hearing Before the Committee on the Judiciary United States Senate: Nomination of Floyd H. Roberts to be United States*

District Judge for the Western District of Virginia, 76th Cong., 1st sess., 1939, S578-9.

124. See *CIS Index to Unpublished U.S. Senate Committee Hearings: 18th Congress to 88th Congress, 1823–1964*, vol. 2, Subject Index N–Z (Bethesda: Congressional Information Service, 1986), 588–630.

125. This oath was actually administered to G. Harrold Carswell in his lower-court nomination and is consequently discussed in some detail in his Supreme Court nomination hearings. See *Hearings Before the Committee on the Judiciary United States Senate: Nomination of George Harrold Carswell, of Florida, to be Associate Justice of the Supreme Court of the United States*, 91st Cong., 2d sess., 1970, 38–40. The transcript of Carswell's original hearing as a district judge, Senate Hearing (85) SJ-T.6, took place on March 26, 1958 and was never published. The oath was also administered to Harry Blackmun at his hearing to be a judge on the U.S. Court of Appeals for the Eighth Circuit; the hearing, also unpublished, took place on September 14, 1959.

126. For a useful account of the deterioration of the process during the Reagan years, see *Scoring Points*, Chapter 5. For a more polemical account, see *Right Wing Justice*, Chapter 2.

127. *Hearings Before the Committee on the Judiciary United States Senate: The Nomination of Ruth Bader Ginsburg, to be Associate Justice of the Supreme Court of the United States*, 103rd Cong., 1st sess., 1993, Senate Hearing 103–432. Hatch's questioning can be found at pages 263–267, Biden's rejoinder at pages 275–276.

128. Biden's questioning of Roberts can be found at http://www.washingtonpost.com/wp-dyn/content/article/2005/09/13/AR2005091300979.html.

129. Hatch devoted nearly the entirety of his opening statement at Roberts's hearing to this point. It can be found at http://www.washingtonpost.com/wp-dyn/content/article/2005/09/13/AR2005091300693.html.

130. See Senate floor speech by Iowa Senator Smith Brookhart, *Congressional Record*, 71st Cong., 2d sess., February 12, 1930. Vol. 72, part 4, 3505.

131. Carter, *The Confirmation Mess*, 205–206.

132. Robert Bork, "Civil Rights—A Challenge," *New Republic*, August 31, 1963, 21. Bork disavowed the article and its argument at his confirmation hearing.

133. See "Federalist No. 51."

Chapter 4

1. See Elisabeth Bumiller, "Focus for Supreme Court Pick Is Said to Be on Diversity," *New York Times*, September 22, 2005, 22; Jan Crawford Greenburg, "Conservatives say Democrats cowed Bush into weak court choice," *Chicago Tribune*, October 9, 2005, 1.
2. Comiskey, *Seeking Justices*, Chapter 4.
3. See *Judging Thomas*, Chapters 15–17.
4. Editorial, "Dangerous Nonsense," *New York Times*, February 27, 1955, E8.
5. See Orrin Hatch, *Square Peg: Confessions of a Citizen Senator* (New York: Basic Books, 2002), 180.
6. Roberts interview.
7. The quotation from Ginsburg's testimony can be found in *Ginsburg Hearings*, 323. Ginsburg made her comments about Roberts's testimony in a speech at Wake Forest University on September 28, 2005.
8. Schumer's opening statement can be found at http://www.washingtonpost.com/wp-dyn/content/article/2005/09/13/AR2005091300693.html.
9. *Stewart Nomination*, 64.
10. *Hearings Before the Committee on the Judiciary United States Senate: The Nomination of Robert H. Bork to be Associate Justice of the Supreme Court of the United States*, 100th Cong., 1st sess., 1987, Senate Hearing 100-1011, part 1. For Bork's comments on *Griswold*, see pages 114–116. For his discussion of *Roe*, see pages 184–185.
11. For Ginsburg's discussions of her criticisms of *Roe*, see *Ginsburg Hearings*, 148–50. For her general view of abortion rights, see 207.
12. Ronald Dworkin, "The Strange Case of Judge Alito," *New York Review of Books*, February 23, 2006, 14.
13. *Ginsburg Hearings*, 264–265.
14. *Hearings Before the Committee on the Judiciary United States Senate: The Nomination of Stephen G. Breyer to be an Associate Justice of the Supreme Court of the United States*, 103rd Cong., 2d sess., 1994, Senate Hearing 103-715, 269. Breyer declined to address with any specificity the parameters of the *Roe* right. See page 138.
15. See, for example, Justice Thomas's dissent in *Stenberg v. Carhart*, 530 U.S. 914 (2000), joined also by Justice Scalia and Chief Justice

Rehnquist: "the *Casey* joint opinion was constructed by its authors out of whole cloth. The standard set forth in the *Casey* joint opinion has no historical or doctrinal pedigree. The standard is a product of its authors' own philosophical views about abortion, and it should go without saying that it has no origins in or relationship to the Constitution and is, consequently, as illegitimate as the standard it purported to replace. Even assuming, however, as I will for the remainder of this dissent, that *Casey's* fabricated undue-burden standard merits adherence (which it does not), today's decision is extraordinary."

16. The court rejected the claimed right to physician-assisted suicide in *Washington v. Glucksberg*, 521 U.S. 702 (1997). It struck down sodomy laws in *Lawrence v. Texas*, 539 U.S. 558 (2003).

17. This is not necessarily the case, of course. It is possible for a conservative jurist who values consistency in the Court's adjudication to believe the *Roe* principle, having been articulated, ought to be given reasonable application in related areas until such time as the Court overturns it. But few conservatives are this principled. A nominee who announced opposition to *Roe* would consequently be understood, probably correctly, to be declaring opposition to *Roe's* extension.

18. *Hearings Before the Committee on the Judiciary United States Senate: The Nomination of Clarence Thomas to be Associate Justice of the Supreme Court of the United States*, 102nd Cong., 1st sess., 1991, Senate Hearing 102-1084 Part 1, 222–223.

19. Ibid. Thomas acknowledges the right to privacy on page 127, argues for the importance of *stare decisis* on pages 246–247, describes his general contentment with commerce clause jurisprudence on pages 374–375, and distances himself from the work of constitutional theorist and property rights enthusiast Richard Epstein on pages 113–116.

20. *Hearing Before the Committee on the Judiciary United States Senate: Nomination of Judge Antonin Scalia, to be Associate Justice of the Supreme Court of the United States*, 99th Cong., 2d sess., 1986, Senate Hearing 99-1064. Scalia's refusal to discuss *Roe* can be found at page 37. His refusal to discuss the right to privacy more generally can be found at pages 101–102. His refusal to discuss *Marbury* can be found at pages 33–34.

21. Blue slips are the modern incarnation of the very old practice of senatorial courtesy, by which the body defers to objections from

individual senators concerning judicial nominations from their states. Under the system, the Judiciary Committee will not typically proceed with a nomination without the consent of both home-state senators, though committee chairmen tend to defer more fully to home-state senators of their own party.

22. Article III, Section 1.
23. See, for example, Steven G. Calabresi, "Stop Talking? Yes," *Legal Times*, May 12, 2003, 60.
24. For an account of nineteenth-century Supreme Court nominations, see *Justices, Presidents, and Senators*, Chapters 5–7.
25. William H. Rehnquist, *Grand Inquests: The Historic Impeachments of Justice Samuel Chase and President Andrew Johnson* (New York: William Morrow and Company, Inc., 1992), 114.
26. *Marshall Hearings*, 197–198.
27. Olson's memo can be found at http://www.washingtonpost.com/wp-srv/nation/documents/olson_04_12_1982.pdf. Roberts's rebuttal can be found at http://www.washingtonpost.com/wp-srv/nation/documents/roberts_appellate_jurisdiction.pdf.
28. The Antiterrorism and Effective Death Penalty Act of 1996 was passed as part of Public Law 104-132, enacted on April 24, 1996. The Illegal Immigration Reform and Immigrant Responsibility Act of 1996 was passed as part of Public Law 104-208, enacted on September 30, 1996.
29. The court asserted jurisdiction over Guantanamo Bay in *Rasul v. Bush*, 542 U.S. 466 (2004). The Detainee Treatment Act of 2005 was enacted as part of the Department of Defense Appropriations Act, 2006, Public Law 109-148, December 30, 2005.
30. See 28 U.S.C. § 2241.
31. The House of Representatives passed the Marriage Protection Act of 2004, H.R. 3313, on July 22 of that year to strip all federal courts of constitutional challenges to the Defense of Marriage Act of 1996, which prohibits federal recognition of same-sex marriages and permits states to refuse recognition of same-sex marriages performed by one another. The same year, on September 23, it passed the Pledge Protection Act of 2004, H.R. 2028, to strip all federal courts of jurisdiction over constitutional challenges to the Pledge of Allegiance or its recitation.
32. See, for example, the Streamlined Procedures Act of 2005, introduced in the Senate as S. 1088 and in the House of Representatives as H.R. 3035.

33. See Public Law No. 109-3.
34. See *Schiavo ex rel. Schindler v. Schiavo*, 357 F. Supp. 2d 1378 (Middle District Fla. 2005). See also *Schiavo ex rel. Schindler v. Schiavo*, 403 F.3d 1223 (11th Cir. 2005), rehearing denied 403 F.3d 1261 (11th Cir. 2005).
35. "Quotes on Terri Schiavo's Death," *Associated Press*, March 31, 2005.
36. Sheryl Gay Stolberg, "Majority Leader Asks House Panel to Review Judges," *New York Times*, April 14, 2005, A1.
37. Information about the conference, sponsored by the Traditional Values Coalition, can be found at http://www.traditionalvalues.org/modules.php?sid=2195. For an account of the event, see Ruth Marcus, "Booting the Bench," *Washington Post*, April 11, 2005, A19.
38. Editorial, "Beyond the Pale," *Washington Post*, April 17, 2005, B6.
39. See Greg Gordon, "Judge Sits in the Middle of Capitol Struggle," *Star Tribune*, March 15, 2003, B1. See also Frederic J. Frommer, "Sensenbrenner Defends Probe of Minnesota Federal Judge," *Associated Press*, March 16, 2004.
40. Charles Lane, "Republicans Investigate Judge in Michigan Case," *Washington Post*, November 1, 2003, A5.
41. See *In re Complaint Against Circuit Judge Richard D. Cudahy*, 294 F.3d 947 (7th Cir. 2002).
42. A copy of the letter can be found at http://www.nacdl.org/public.nsf/mediasources/20050711a/$FILE/Sensenbrenner.pdf.
43. See, for example, the House Judiciary Committee press release "House Approves Legislation Allowing States to Decide Whether 'Under God' Should Remain in the Pledge of Allegiance, September 23, 2004, in which Sensenbrenner says: "To protect the Pledge from federal court decisions that would have the effect of invalidating the Pledge across several states, or nationwide, H.R. 2028 will reserve to the state courts the authority to decide whether the Pledge is valid within each state's boundaries. It will place final authority over a state's Pledge policy in the hands of the states themselves. If different states come to different decisions regarding the constitutionality of the Pledge, the effects of such decisions will be felt only within those states. A few federal judges sitting hundreds of miles away from your state will not be able to rewrite your state's Pledge policy." The release can be found at http://judiciary.house.gov/newscenter.aspx?A=335. A similar one concerning the Marriage

Protection Act can be found at http://judiciary.house.gov/
newscenter.aspx?A=200.

Chapter 5

1. *Gonzales v. Oregon*, 126 S. Ct. 904 (2006).
2. See, for example, E.J. Dionne Jr., "Bad Law, Good Ruling," *Washington Post*, January 20, 2006, A17.
3. The text of President Bush's speech on the subject can be found at http://www.whitehouse.gov/news/releases/2002/10/20021030-6.html.
4. See, for example, *Congressional Record*, 105th Cong., 1st sess., March 19, 1997. Vol. 143, no. 36, S2516-S2517.
5. Richard Davis, *Electing Justice: Fixing the Supreme Court Nomination Process* (Oxford: Oxford University Press, 2005), 170–178.
6. Carter, *The Confirmation Mess*, 203–204.
7. See, for example, Calvin R. Massey, "Getting There: A Brief History of the Politics of Supreme Court Appointments," Hastings Constitutional Law Quarterly 19 (1991): 1; Gary J. Simson, "Thomas's Supreme Unfitness—A Letter to the Senate on Advise and Consent," Cornell Law Review 78 (1993): 619. *Seeking Justices* contains a sober discussion on pages 189–191.
8. Rehnquist spoke publicly about the mistreatment of President Clinton's nominees in his 1997 Year-End Report on the Federal Judiciary: "Whatever the size of the federal judiciary, the President should nominate candidates with reasonable promptness, and the Senate should act within a reasonable time to confirm or reject them. Some current nominees have been waiting a considerable time for a Senate Judiciary Committee vote or a final floor vote. The Senate confirmed only 17 judges in 1996 and 36 in 1997, well under the 101 judges it confirmed during 1994."
9. Benjamin Wittes, "Confirmation Class: Most of what we learn from confirmation hearings for a Supreme Court chief justice will be misleading or irrelevant," *Atlantic Monthly*, April 1, 2005, 38.
10. Alito hearing transcript, 12 January 2006, available at: http://www.washingtonpost.com/wp-dyn/content/article/2006/01/12/AR2006011201473.html.
11. Souter may have simply been more verbose than Thomas, who merely stated his belief that the right to privacy existed, but he explained in some detail the constitutional history from which he derives the right. See *Hearings Before the Committee on the Judiciary United States Senate: The Nomination of David H. Souter to be*

Associate Justice of the Supreme Court of the United States, 101st Cong., 2d sess., 1990, Senate Hearing 101-1263, 54–59.

12. Anthony Lewis, "Respecting the Court," *New York Times*, September 21, 1990, A31. Both the *New York Times* and *Washington Post* expressed some measure of relief in editorials following his testimony as well. See Editorial, "For David Souter, With Hope," *New York Times*, September 27, 1990, 22; Editorial, "Judge Souter as Witness," *Washington Post*, September 20, 1990, A22.

13. Janet Malcolm, "The Art of Testifying: The Confirmation Hearings as Theatre," *New Yorker*, March 13, 2006, 70–79.

14. Editorial, "The Rehnquist Nomination," *Washington Post*, September 12, 1986, A22.

15. Comiskey, *Seeking Justices*, Chapter 6.

16. *Bork Hearings*, 423, 428.

17. *Frankfurter Hearings*, 107.

18. Maltese, *The Selling of Supreme Court Nominees*, 10.

19. Carter, *The Confirmation Mess*, 193.

20. Alito hearing transcript, 9 January 2006, available at http://www .washingtonpost.com/wp-dyn/content/article/2006/01/09/AR2006010 900755.html.

21. Roberts interview.

22. *Justices, Presidents, and Senators*, Chapters 5–7.

23. The vocabulary of a "broken" system in need of "fixing" is pervasive in discussion of the nominations process. For example, Richard Davis's book *Electing Justice* uses the subtitle "Fixing the Supreme Court Nomination Process"; the introduction is entitled "A Broken Process."

INDEX

■

abortion rights, advocates of, 31; constitutional protection of, 95–96
Abraham, Henry J., 49; black appointment inevitable from, 73; Brandeis confirmation battle comments by, 45–46
academic credentials, 40–41
Adams, John Quincy, 1, 16
affirmative action, 31
African Americans, judge inevitable, 73; Marshall, as first judge, 54; voting rights for, 147n42
Alito, Samuel A., 1, 6, 20, 89, 92, 100, 112, 119
American civil liberties, 63
American constitutional system, 63
American Federation of Labor, 51
American politics, confirmation process and, 13–14; courts fought over in, 4; judicial authority in, 81–82
Americans, judges beliefs important to, 59; judicial power admired by, 82,

112; Republican control from, 128–29
Ashcroft, John, 8, 43

Bayh, Birch, 77
the bench. *See* judiciary
Biden, Joseph, 79, 119
Bingham, John, 74
Black, Charles, Jr., 57
blacks. *See* African Americans
"blue slip" procedure, 101, 141n13, 155n21
Borah, William, 49
Bork, Robert, 18; Brandeis nomination difference with, 47; Supreme Court comments by, 21, 137n5; Supreme Court scathed by, 24
Brandeis, Louis, 44; Bork nomination difference with, 47; confirmation battle intense for, 45–46; Senate process opened up with, 48
Brennan, William, 23, 43, 68, 122

questioning, 79; senators'
questioning, 75–76
Constitution, powers of, 138n7;
presidents' power from, 145n14;
Senate's role from, 104–5;
separation of powers with, 84–85;
Supreme Court's budget and, 105
constitutional guarantee, 103–4
constitutional instruments, 130
constitutional law, 17, 105
constitutional protection, 95–96
"Constitution in Exile" movement, 30
Coolidge, Calvin, 42
"courtesy calls," 3
court of appeals, 90
courts, American politics fighting over,
4; close relatives serving on,
139n11; Congress reining in, 108;
conservative, 49; liberals' viewpoint
on, 30–31; policy range of, 60; as
political institution, 21–22; role of,
21
court-stripping measures, 106; Congress
passing, 107; constitutional law and,
105
CRS. *See* Congressional Research
Service
Cudahy, Richard, 109

Davis, Richard, 116
D.C. Circuit court, 40
death penalty, 79
"decency," 33–34
DeLay, Tom, 108
"democratic moment," 124–25
Democrats, blue slips used by, 141n13;
judicial nominees view by, 28;
judicial nominee treatment by, 22;
Senate controlled by, 38–39
denial argument, caution from, 20;
virtue of, 17–18
desegregation, 66
doctor-assisted suicide, 113
Douglas, William O., 30, 106
Dred Scott, 59

Durham, Barbara, 139n12
Dworkin, Ronald, 96

Easterbrook, Frank, 109
Eastland, James, Harlan comments
from, 66; judicial nominees'
philosophy probed by, 69–70;
question motives of, 67
Eisenhower, Dwight, 28, 146n16
Eisler, Kim Isaac, 69
Electing Justice (Davis), 116
environmental protection, 31
Epstein, Lee, 15
Ervin, Sam, judicial philosophy,
platitudes of, 70; Marshall frustrates,
75
Estrada, Miguel, 88; complex views of,
8; nomination circumstances of, 44–
45; senators demanding response
from, 32
executive branch, 118

federal courts, 110
"Federalist No. 51," 114
federal judges, 109
federal judiciary, high-court percentage
of, 7; transforming, 27
federal power revisions, 30
filibuster, 40, 113, 141n14
First Amendment, 24, 83
Fletcher, Betty Binns, 8
Fletcher, William, 8, 20
Fong, Hiram, 70
Ford, Gerald, 38
Fortas, Abe, 55–56, 70
Fourteenth Amendment, 69, 73–74
Frankfurter, Felix, 23; allegations
against, 62–63; McCarran exchange
with, 63–64
Friendly, Henry, 74

Garland, Merrick, 40, 115
Ginsburg, Ruth Bader, 28, 44, 79, 97
Glenn, Otis, 50
Goldberg, Arthur, 70
Gorton, Slade, 8